MACMILLAN
McGRAW-HILL

W9-AOC-743

Science

Activity
Resources

**Macmillan
McGraw-Hill**

Grade 3

Cover: Tom and Pat Leeson, photo; bamboo border—Roderick Chen/Superstock.
Title page: Roderick Chen/Superstock.

The McGraw·Hill Companies

Macmillan
McGraw-Hill

Table of Contents

What Are the Features of Living Things?

Hypothesize What features do you think living things have? How could you test your ideas?

Write a **Hypothesis:**

Possible hypothesis: Living things grow, develop, and reproduce. Test that living things grow and develop by germinating a seed.

Materials

- 25 pea seeds
- 25 pieces of gravel (pea-sized)
- hand lens
- 2 plastic cups
- piece of white paper
- teaspoon
- water

Procedure

1. **Measure** Work with a partner. Place one teaspoon of pea seeds on the white paper. Place one teaspoon of gravel next to the pea seeds.

2. **Observe** Look at the seeds and gravel with the hand lens. Compare the seeds and the gravel. Record your observations.

   The pea seeds are green, wrinkled, hard and dry. The gravel is hard and dry, and different shapes and colors. Both appear lifeless.

3. Mark a plastic cup A. Place the seeds in it. Mark the other plastic cup B. Place the gravel in it. Pour the same amount of water into each cup. Make sure the seeds and gravel are completely covered with water.

4. **Predict** What do you think will happen after two days?

   Possible answer: The seeds will sprout and the gravel will not.

5. **Observe** Look at the soaked seeds and gravel every few hours for two days. Record your observations.

   The seeds swell and sprout. The gravel does not change.

Drawing Conclusions

1. What is the living thing? How do you know?

   Possible answers: The seeds are living things. The seeds sprouted.

   _____

2. Infer What are some features of living things?

   Possible answer: Living things grow and change.

   _____

3. FURTHER INQUIRY **Infer** Are you a living thing? How do you know?

   Possible answer: Yes, I am growing and changing.

   _____

Inquiry

Think of your own questions that you might test. How can you tell if other things are alive?

My Question Is:

Possible question: Are cooked peas living things?

_____

How I Can Test It:

Possible test: Observe a cooked pea to see if it is growing and changing. Try to

germinate the cooked pea.

My Results Are:

Possible answer: Cooked peas are not living things.

©Macmillan/McGraw-Hill

Is Yeast Alive?

Procedure

BE CAREFUL! Wear goggles.

1. Observe the yeast and record your observations.

   Possible answer: The yeast is a grayish white solid and it
   does not move.

2. Predict whether or not the yeast is alive. Record your prediction.

   Possible answer: The yeast is not alive.

3. Fill a glass halfway with warm water. Place one-half teaspoon of yeast and one-half teaspoon of sugar in the glass of water.

4. Wait 30 minutes. Observe the yeast and touch the side of the glass. Record your observations.

   The glass will be warm and the yeast will give off carbon dioxide gas in the form of bubbles.

Drawing Conclusions

1. Explain your prediction in step 2.

   Possible answer: The yeast did not move or respond when I touched it, so it could not be alive.

2. Based on your observations, was your prediction correct? Explain your answer.

   Possible answer: No. The yeast responded to the water, a change in its environment, so it must be alive.

How Many Cells?

Hypothesize How many cells are on your hand?

Write a **Hypothesis:**

Possible hypothesis: A cell is so small that many cells fit inside an ink dot.

Materials

- pen
- beans
- paper

Procedure

1. **Predict** On a separate piece of paper, trace around your hand. Make the smallest dot you can on the hand. Write down the number of cells you think it covers?

   Possible answer: Students may predict any number. A prediction might be 100.

2. **Use Numbers** Make a circle. This circle represents the ink dot on the hand. Fill the circle with beans. How many beans did you use?

   Possible answer: Each group should have about 500 beans.

Drawing Conclusions

3. **Interpret Data** Each bean represents a skin cell. How many skin cells are under the ink dot?

   Student answers will vary. Possible answer: There are approximately 500 skin cells under the ink dot.

4. How did your prediction compare to this number? Record your answer.

   Students answers will vary. Possible answer: My prediction was low.

© Macmillan/McGraw-Hill

5. Going Further Are different types of cells the same size and shape? Design and conduct an experiment to find out.

My Hypothesis Is:

Possible hypothesis: Different types of cells are different sizes and shapes.

_____

My Experiment Is:

Possible experiment: Place an onion leaf on a glass slide and view it under a microscope. Draw what you see. Next, take a drop of pond water and place it on a glass slide and view it under a microscope. Draw what you see.

My Results Are:

Plant cells are usually boxlike whereas animal cells come in a variety of shapes, and are often rounded. Plant cells are usually larger than animal cells.

Experiment

How Does a Mealworm Respond to Its Environment?

In this activity you will experiment to find out how a mealworm responds to changes in its environment.

Procedure **BE CAREFUL!** Handle animals with care.

Wash hands after handling mealworms.

1. **Observe** Look at the mealworm with the hand lens. How does it move? Very gently, touch it with a toothpick. Record your observations.

   Possible observations: The mealworm curls up.

   _____

2. Plan several ways to change the mealworm's environment. Be sure the changes will not harm it. Record your plans in the chart below.

3. **Experiment** Test the statements. Record your results. Repeat the experiment. Compare these results to those recorded on the chart.

If Statement	Then Statement	Results
if something gets in the mealworm's path	then it will change its path	Yes, it changed its path.
If . . . Possible Answer: I place a drop of water on the paper	then . . . Possible Answer: the mealworm will crawl toward it.	Possible Result: Yes, the mealworm crawled toward it.

© Macmillan/McGraw-Hill

Drawing Conclusions

How does the mealworm respond to changes in its environment?

Possible answer: When I placed the ruler in the mealworm's path, it changed

direction. Additional sentences will vary depending on the changes to the

environment tested.

_____

_____

_____

©Macmillan/McGraw-Hill

What Do Plants Need?

Hypothesize What things do you think plants need to live? How can you test your ideas?

Write a **Hypothesis:**

Possible hypothesis: Plants need water and light to live.

_____

_____

Materials

- soaked pea seeds from Lesson 1
- 6 half-pint cartons
- $4\frac{1}{2}$ cups of soil
- water
- water with nutrients
- metric ruler

Procedure

1. **Measure** Place $\frac{3}{4}$ cup of soil in each carton. Plant the seeds, and cover them with a thin layer of soil.

2. Label the cartons *Light, Water, Nutrients, No Light, No Water,* and *No Nutrients.*

3. Put the carton labeled *No Light* in a dark place. Put the remaining cartons in a sunny area. Water the cartons labeled *Light, No Light, Water,* and *No Nutrients.* Water the carton labeled *Nutrients* with water containing nutrients.

4. **Measure** Look at the plants. Measure and record the height of each plant twice a week. Record what you see in the table below.

Plants	Day 1	Day 4	Day 8	Day 12
Light				
Water				
Nutrients				
No light				
No water				
No nutrients				

©Macmillan/McGraw-Hill

Drawing Conclusions

1. Which plants are the healthiest after two weeks? How do you know?

The plants that received the light and water should look the healthiest.

_____

2. What do seeds need to grow into healthy plants?

light, water, and soil

_____

3. FURTHER INQUIRY **Infer** What else do you think plants need to survive? Explain your answer.

Possible answers should include air.

_____

Inquiry

Think of your own questions you might test. Do plants need to grow in warm temperatures?

My Question Is:

Possible question: Can a plant live in a cold environment?

_____

How Can I Test It:

Possible test: Take two plants. Put one in a cold spot. Put another in a warm spot.

Make sure each plant gets sunlight and water.

My Results Are:

Answers will vary depending on the type of plants used and the temperature.

Many houseplants will not do well in very cold temperatures.

What Plants Need

Procedure

Materials

- 2 potted pea plants about 2 weeks old

1. Place one of the pea plants in a sunny spot on the windowsill. Place the second pea plant in a dark closet.

2. Predict what might happen to the pea plant in the closet.

   The pea plant in the closet will stop growing.

3. Water both plants the same amount each day.

4. After several days, compare the two pea plants. Record your comparisons.

   The pea plant on the sunny windowsill is much larger than the plant in the dark closet.

Drawing Conclusions

1. What happened to the pea plant in the closet? Explain.

   The leaves begin to dry out and turn brown. The leaves need sunlight to grow.

2. What might happen if you kept both plants where they are for another week?

   The pea plant on the windowsill would grow bigger. The pea plant in the closet would die without sunlight.

© Macmillan/McGraw-Hill

Water Moves in a Plant

Hypothesize How does water travel through a plant?

Write a **Hypothesis:**

Possible hypothesis: Plants absorb water with their roots.

The water travels from the roots, through the stem, and to

the leaves.

Materials

- clear plastic glass
- 1 celery stalk with leaves
- 1 white carnation with leaves
- food coloring
- water

Procedure **BE CAREFUL!** Wear goggles.

1. **Measure** Put about 5 cm (2 in.) of water in a clear plastic glass. Add about ten drops of food coloring.

2. **Predict** Put a freshly cut celery stalk in the cup for two hours. What do you think will happen? *May also use a fresh flower (carnation, white color works well also.)*

   Possible answer: The colored water will move up through the celery stalk.

Drawing Conclusions

3. **Observe** What did you observe after 2 hours? Write and draw your answer.

   Possible answer: The celery stalk slowly changed color starting at the bottom

   of the stem and finishing at the leaves.

4. **Infer** How does water travel through a plant?

   Possible answer: Water is drawn up the stem to the leaves.

©Macmillan/McGraw-Hill

QUICK LAB
FOR SCHOOL OR HOME
Lesson 2

5. Going Further Do you think light affects how fast water travels through a plant? Design and conduct an experiment to find out.

My Hypothesis Is:

Possible answer: Light does not affect how fast water travels through a plant.

_____

My Experiment Is:

Put a celery stalk in a glass and place it in a dark area. Put a second stalk in a

glass and place it in the light.

_____

_____

My Results Are:

Possible answer: My hypothesis was correct.

_____

How Does a Plant's Life Begin?

Hypothesize How does a plant's life begin? How could you test your ideas?

Write a **Hypothesis:**

Possible hypothesis: A plant starts life as a seed. This

hypothesis can be tested by planting a seed and observing

what happens.

Procedure

1. **Observe** Look at the seeds with a hand lens.

   The seeds are green or tan, wrinkled, hard, dry, and

   appear lifeless.

2. Place the seeds in the cup, and cover them with water. Soak the seeds overnight.

3. **Observe** Look at a seed with the hand lens.

   Possible answer: The seeds have softened and swelled.

4. Use the toothpick to separate the two halves of the seed. Use the hand lens to observe each half. Draw what you see.

   Possible answer: A small shoot and root are visible when the seed is split

   in half.

5. Moisten a folded paper towel, and place it inside the plastic bag. Place the other four seeds at the bottom of the plastic bag on top of the paper towel. Seal the bag.

Materials

- 5 pea seeds
- hand lens
- plastic cup
- $\frac{1}{4}$ cup of water
- paper towel
- self-sealing plastic bag, pint-sized
- toothpick

©Macmillan/McGraw-Hill

6. Observe Observe the seeds each day. Record your observations.

Possible observation: The seeds sprouted within 3 days.

_____

_____

Drawing Conclusions

1. How did the seeds change after they were soaked? What did you find between the two halves of the seed?

The seeds became larger and softer. A tiny plant was visible inside the seed.

_____

2. **FURTHER INQUIRY** **Infer** Which seed part provides food for the young plant as it grows from a seed? Design and conduct an experiment to test your ideas.

Food is contained inside the seed.

Inquiry

Think of your own questions that you might test. Do all plants follow the same stages of development?

My Question Is:

Possible question: Do nasturtiums or sunflowers follow the same stages of

development as a pea?

How I Can Test It:

Possible test: Plant these seeds and observe their growth.

My Results Are:

Possible answer: Yes, they go through similar stages.

More Seeds

Procedure

Materials

- different types of seeds such as apple, corn, and beans
- water
- plastic cup
- paper towel

1. Place different types of seeds in a plastic cup.

2. Fill the cup with water. Let the cup sit where it will not be disturbed overnight.

3. Carefully drain only the water from the cup.

4. Place the seeds on a paper towel.

5. With your fingers, carefully take apart each seed.

6. Observe the different parts of each seed. Draw and label them in the space below. Drawings should show that each seed has a tiny plant, stored food, and an outer coat.

Drawing Conclusions

Compare the parts of the different kinds of seeds.

Answers should reflect that all the seeds have a tiny plant, stored food, and an outer coat.

_____

_____

QUICK LAB
FOR SCHOOL OR HOME
Lesson 3

Light or Shade?

Hypothesize Does a seedling need light to germinate? How can you test your ideas?

Write a **Hypothesis:**

Possible answer: Seedlings need sunlight. One kept in light will grow better than one kept in darkness.

Materials

- two plastic cups and seedlings from the Explore Activity
- black paper
- paper towels

Procedure

1. Gather two plastic cups and the seedlings from the Explore Activity.

2. Cover the outside of one cup with black paper.

3. Wet some paper towels, and place one in each cup. Put a seedling on the paper towel.

4. Place both cups on a sunny windowsill. Place a piece of black paper over the top of the cup covered with paper. Make sure the towels are kept wet.

● **Drawing Conclusions**

5. **Observe** Look at the seedlings after two days.
Record what happened.

The covered seedling was much smaller. The one in the sunlight was larger.

_____

6. **Infer** What does this tell you about a seedling's needs?

Seedlings need sunlight to grow well.

_____

7. **Going Further** What is the best temperature for a seedling to grow?
Design and conduct an experiment to find out.

My Hypothesis Is:

Possible answer: A seedling will grow the best when it is in a

warm environment.

My Experiment Is:

Possible answer: Put one cup with a seedling in it in a warm place. Put one

cup with a seedling in a very cold place. Water each seedling and make sure

they both get enough light.

_____

_____

My Results Are:

Possible answer: Seedlings will do better in warmer temperatures and will

not grow in temperatures below freezing.

What Do Animals Need to Live and Grow?

Hypothesize What do you think animals need to live and grow? How could you test your ideas?

Write a **Hypothesis:**

Possible hypothesis: Animals need food, water, light, and
air. This hypothesis can be tested by observing an animal.

Materials

- small plastic cup with lid

- caterpillar

- food for the caterpillar

- hand lens

- teaspoon

Procedure **BE CAREFUL!** Handle animals with care.

Wash your hands after handling caterpillars.

1. Place the caterpillar food in the bottom of the plastic cup.

2. Carefully put the caterpillar in the cup. Cover the cup with the lid.

3. Place the caterpillar in a cool place out of the sunlight.

4. **Observe** Look at the caterpillar once a day for two weeks. Record what you see.

   Possible observations: The caterpillar is eating, growing, and
   excreting waste.

© Macmillan/McGraw-Hill

Drawing Conclusions

1. How did your caterpillar change during the two weeks?

   Possible answer: The caterpillar grew and excreted waste. It molted and

   changed into a pupa.

2. What happened to the food?

   Possible answer: The caterpillar ate the food.

3. What do caterpillars need to live and grow?

   Possible answer: food, the right temperature, shelter, and air.

4. **FURTHER INQUIRY** **Experiment** How could you test to see if another living thing does the same things as the caterpillar at different times in its life?

   Possible answer: Students might suggest that they observe another

   developing animal, such as a puppy or kitten, and keep a record of

   their observations.

Inquiry

Think of your own questions that you might test. Do all animals need the same things as a caterpillar?

My Question Is:

Do I need the same things as a caterpillar?

How I Can Test It:

List my daily needs and compare them to a caterpillar's needs.

My Results Are:

We all need food, water, shelter, and air to live.

© Macmillan/McGraw-Hill

What You Need to Live

Procedure

1. Record in a notebook what you need to live. Keep track for an entire day.

2. In your notebook, make a list showing what you needed.

3. Make another list showing what a pet of your choice needs to live.

4. Compare the two lists.

Drawing Conclusions

1. What things do you need in order to live?

   Possible answer: I need water, different types of food, the right temperature, sunlight, exercise, clothes, and shelter.

2. What does the pet need to live?

   The pet needs food, water, exercise, and shelter.

3. How are your needs and the pet's needs alike? How are they different?

   We both need water, exercise, and food. The pet needs a simpler place to live than I do. The pet doesn't need sunlight to grow or clothes for protection like I do.

© Macmillan/McGraw-Hill

QUICK LAB
FOR SCHOOL OR HOME
Lesson 4

Food Is a Fuel

Hypothesize What food groups do you eat from everyday? How can you find out?

Write a **Hypothesis:**

Possible answer: I eat from all the food groups.
_____

_____

Procedure

1. **Predict** Do you eat something from every food group most days?

   Yes, I eat from every food group.
   _____

2. For each of the next three days, record everything that you eat.

3. **Interpret Data** Next to each item on your list, write the name of the food group it belongs to.

	Food	Food Group
Day 1		
Day 2		
Day 3		

©Macmillan/McGraw-Hill

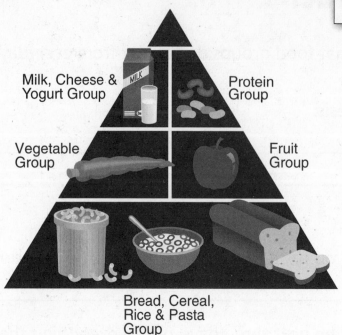

Milk, Cheese &
Yogurt Group

Protein
Group

Vegetable
Group

Fruit
Group

Bread, Cereal,
Rice & Pasta
Group

Drawing Conclusions

4. Did you eat something from every food group? Compare your results with your classmates'.

   <u>Most students eat from each group, but may be surprised at how much they</u>

   <u>eat from one or two groups compared to the other groups.</u>

5. **Going Further** How many servings from each food group did you eat each day? Do you need to eat more of some food groups and less than others? Which ones? Record your findings.

   <u>Answers will vary depending on the foods eaten. Students should make</u>

   <u>recommendations about how many more or how many less servings they</u>

   <u>should include for each group.</u>

   _____

   _____

How Does a Caterpillar Change As It Grows?

Hypothesize How does a caterpillar change over its lifetime? How could you find out?

Write a **Hypothesis:**

Possible hypothesis: A caterpillar grows and changes into a

butterfly. Observe a caterpillar's life cycle.

Materials

- caterpillar and container from Lesson 4

- hand lens

Procedure **BE CAREFUL!** Handle animals with care.

1. **Observe** Look at the caterpillar with the hand lens. Make a drawing of it.

2. **Observe** Look at the caterpillar each day for two weeks. Record your findings. Include a drawing of what the caterpillar looks like.

3. How has the caterpillar changed?

The caterpillar eats and grows. It molts several times, and eats the skin

it sheds. After 7 to 10 days, the caterpillar spins a silk pad on the lid,

attaches to the pad, hangs upside down, and molts a final time revealing

the pupa. The pupa has a hard protective coating. In 7 to 10 days the

butterfly emerges.

© Macmillan/McGraw-Hill

Drawing Conclusions

1. What happened to the caterpillar?

   The caterpillar grew and changed into pupa and then into a butterfly.

2. What does the caterpillar become when it is an adult?

   Possible answer: The caterpillar changes into a butterfly.

3. **Classify** In what ways are the young and adult forms different?

   A caterpillar has a worm-like body with a jaw for chewing. A butterfly has

   colorful wings, long antennae, three pairs of legs, and a tube-shaped mouth.

4. **FURTHER INQUIRY** **Communicate** Which animal seems to change more—the caterpillar or a dog? How do you know?

   The caterpillar because you can see the different stages of growth.

Inquiry

Think of your own questions that you might test. Do all animals go through the same stages of development?

My Question Is:

Possible question: Do frogs go through the same stages of

development as butterflies?

How I Can Test It:

Possible test: Observe tadpoles change into frogs.

My Results Are:

Possible answer: Frogs go through different stages of development.

©Macmillan/McGraw-Hill

Drawing Butterflies

Procedure

1. Look at the drawings of the stages in the life of a butterfly.

2. On your desk, place the stages in the order they occur.

3. Label the stages from 1 to 4, with 1 being the first stage.

4. List and describe the stages.

   1. Egg is small and shaped like an oval.

   2. Larva or caterpillar is a hairy, worm-like organism with many colors.

   3. Pupa is a brownish, hard case.

   4. Adult butterfly has two wings with several colors, a body, and a head.

Materials

- drawings of stages in the life of a butterfly

Drawing Conclusions

Explain why you placed the stages in the order you did.

Possible answer: Eggs are the smallest, so they must be the first stage. Each stage

increases in size until the largest, the adult butterfly, forms.

© Macmillan/McGraw-Hill

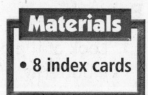

Name That Trait!

Hypothesize What traits do you think you inherited from your parents? What things did you learn? Make a list for each.

Write a **Hypothesis:**

Possible hypothesis: You may inherit your eye color, hair color, and height from your parents. You may learn a language, manners, and customs from your parents.

Materials

• 8 index cards

Procedure   Students will work in pairs. Each student will need 4 index cards.

1. On each of two index cards, write a trait that can be inherited. On each of two other cards, write a trait that can be learned. Do not show your partner what you write.   Answers will vary. Possible answer for inherited traits: Eye color and hair color. Possible answer for learned traits: language, manners, and customs.

2. Take turns holding up a card. Ask your partner to identify the trait as inherited or learned.

Drawing Conclusions

3. **Classify** Sort the cards into two groups.

4. **Communicate** Make more trait cards. Explain if each trait is learned or inherited.

©Macmillan/McGraw-Hill

What Are the Parts of an Insect?

Hypothesize What is the job of an organism's outer covering? How could you test this idea?

Write a **Hypothesis:**

Possible hypothesis: Body coverings help protect organisms

from weather and enemies. Test this idea by observing

different organisms.

Materials

- caterpillar in a 5-inch clear plastic petri dish
- hand lens
- sheet of white paper
- toothpick
- paper towels

Procedure **BE CAREFUL!** Handle animals with care.

Wash your hands after handling caterpillars.

1. Work with a partner. Cover your work area with a piece of white paper.

2. **Observe** Look at the caterpillar. What parts do you see? Draw the caterpillar.

3. **Observe** Use the hand lens to look at the caterpillar. Draw the parts you see now.

Answers will vary.

_____

_____

4. **Experiment** Use the toothpick to touch the caterpillar gently. How does it move when it is touched?

Possible answer: The caterpillar moves using its legs on the underside of

its body.

Drawing Conclusions

1. What are the parts of a caterpillar?

The parts are body and legs.

2. How does a caterpillar use its parts?

It uses its legs for moving from place to place and its body to sense and

respond to changes in its environment.

3. FURTHER INQUIRY Predict What parts do you think are inside the caterpillar? Research to check your prediction.

Answers will vary. Students may suggest parts to digest food, heart, and

blood vessels, and so on.

Inquiry

Think of your own questions that you might test. What are the parts of other animals? Do all animals have the same parts?

My Question Is:

Possible question: Do all animals have a head and legs?

_____

How I Can Test It:

Possible test: Examine many different kinds of animals.

My Results Are:

Possible answer: Some animals do not have a head (starfish). Some do not have

legs (snakes).

© Macmillan/McGraw-Hill

Living Things Outside

Procedure

1. As a class, go outside. List six living things that you observe.

   Possible answers: grass, bird, cat, tree, flower, squirrel,

   fly, worm

2. On a separate piece of paper, draw at least one plant that you observe. Label the parts you draw.

   Students' drawings will vary. Labeled parts should include leaves, stems,

   branches, and roots.

3. On a separate piece of paper, draw at least one animal that you observe. Label the parts you draw.

   Students' drawings will vary. Labeled parts might include legs, eyes, ears,

   and wings.

Drawing Conclusions

1. What are the parts of the plant you drew? How does the plant use each part?

   Possible answer: The roots take in water and minerals from the soil. The

   stem transports water and minerals to other parts. The leaves make food.

2. What are the parts of the animal you drew? How does the animal use each part?

   Possible answer: The legs move the animal. The eyes enable the animal to

   see. The ears enable the animal to hear.

Classify

Comparing Animals

Classifying information helps you make sense of the world. How can classifying animals help you understand them?

Procedure

1. List ten different animals. You may wish to find pictures of the animals in magazines or other reference materials.

   Possible answer: ant, bear, clam, fish, moose, robin, snail, snake, squirrel, walrus
   _____

2. **Classify** Think of a way to divide the animals into groups. For example, one way is body covers. Give each group a name that explains what the group members have in common.

3. **Communicate** List the name of the group and its members in the table.

Way of Classifying	Groups	Animals in Groups
First way of classifying: body covers	hair	bear, moose, walrus, squirrel
	scales	fish, snake
	feathers	robin
	hard shell	ant, clam, snail
Second way of classifying:		
Third way of classifying:		

4. Think of another way to group the same animals. Repeat steps 2 and 3 two more times.

Drawing Conclusions

1. **Interpret Data** Is there only one way to classify animals? Explain your answer.

   No. There are many ways: body covering, means of movement, body structure, number of legs, and so on.

2. **Communicate** How did you decide how to group the animals?

   Possible answer: Answers will vary: by body coverings, legs, ways of getting air, and so on.

© Macmillan/McGraw-Hill

How Are Animals Classified?

Hypothesize What characteristics would you use to classify animals? How can you test your ideas?

Write a **Hypothesis:**

If students completed the Inquiry Skill Builder on text p. A66,

they might suggest body coverings, legs, ways of getting air,

and so on.

Materials

• research materials

Procedure

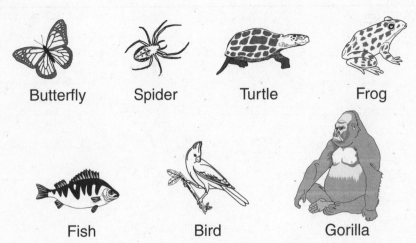

Butterfly   Spider   Turtle   Frog

Fish   Bird   Gorilla

1. **Classify** Look at these animals. How are they alike? How are they different?

   Possible answer: Alike: They all have two eyes and take in oxygen;

   Different: Some animals have wings, some have legs.

2. Divide the animals into two groups. What characteristics did you use to group your animals? Record your answer.

   Focus students on characteristics that scientists might use to classify animals,

   such as body coverings, movement, body parts, methods of obtaining food,

   and habitat.

3. Repeat step 2 three more times. Choose different categories.

● **Drawing Conclusions**

1. What groups did you divide the animals into?

   Students might divide the animals into those that live in water (frog, fish)
   and those that do not (butterfly, spider, turtle, bird, gorilla).

2. What can you conclude about these animals?

   Students should conclude that some of the animals share certain
   characteristics, whereas other animals are very different from each other.

3. **FURTHER INQUIRY** Communicate Can you think of a different system for classifying animals? How would this system be different from the one above?

   Answers will vary based on the criteria for grouping that students used
   above. Some may suggest the kinds of food the animals eat and how long
   they live.

●

Inquiry

Choose one animal on this page. Make a list of questions you might ask about it. Use research materials to find the answers.

Possible questions include: Where does the animal live? How does it get its
food? What does it eat? How does it move? How does it breathe? How does
it reproduce?

Classifying Buttons

Procedure

Materials

• boxes of buttons (different colors, sizes, shapes)

1. With a partner, list some characteristics of the buttons.

   Possible answers could include: Shiny, dull, colorful, round, square, rough, smooth, and so on.

2. Separate the buttons into different groups.

3. Draw the different groups you make on the back of this sheet of paper. Number your groups. Answers will vary.

Drawing Conclusions

1. For each numbered group, what characteristics did you use to group the buttons?

   Possible answers: The buttons were grouped by color, size, texture, material, or shape.

2. Name other objects that you could group like you did the buttons.

   Possible answers: Rocks, seashells, leaves, seeds.

©Macmillan/McGraw-Hill

Name that Animal!

Hypothesize What facts do you need to know about an animal to identify it?

Write a **Hypothesis:**

Possible answers: body covering, how it gets oxygen, warm- or cold-blooded, and so on

Procedure

1. Write the name of a different animal on each of five index cards. List the names here that you will write.

   Possible answers: ostrich, frog, snake. Students may include mammals from page A74 in the pupil text.

2. Trade your cards with another team.

3. One player picks a card. The other player asks yes or no questions about the animal. For example, does the animal have fur? Does it fly?

4. Continue playing until the animal is guessed. Count how many guesses were needed. Record the number below.

Guesses

What Can You Find in an Ecosystem?

Hypothesize Why do organisms live where they do?
Write a **Hypothesis:**

Possible hypothesis: Organisms live in places where they can

obtain the things they need to live and grow.

Materials
- meter tape
- ball of yarn
- 4 clothespins
- hand lens

Procedure

1. **Measure** Mark off an area of ground that is 1 meter square. Stick a clothespin into the ground at each corner. Wrap yarn around the tops of the clothespins.

2. **Observe** Use your hand lens to look at the living and nonliving things in this area.

3. Use the chart to record what you see. Label each object *living* or *nonliving*. Answers will vary depending upon plants and animals selected.

Living Things	Nonliving Things

4. Share your findings with a classmate. Compare the environments each of you observed.

© Macmillan/McGraw-Hill

Explore
Activity
Lesson 1

● **Drawing Conclusions**

1. How many different kinds of nonliving things are in your environment? What did you have the most of?

   Answers will vary depending on the environment chosen.

   _____

2. Choose one living thing you observed. What are the characteristics of this organism?

   Answers will vary.

   _____

3. FURTHER INQUIRY Infer What are the characteristics of another living thing that might live here? How do you know?

   Answers will vary. Each living thing must be able to obtain food, oxygen,

   and water from the environment. Accept all reasonable responses.

●

Inquiry

Think of your own questions that you might like to test. What kinds of organisms live in your environment?

My Question Is:

Possible question: What are the characteristics of the plants and animals

that live around me?

How I Can Test It:

Possible answer: I can make a list of the plants and animals that I

observe around me. Then I can list their characteristics.

My Results Are:

Answers will vary depending upon environment.

_____

●

Alternative Explore
Lesson 1

Sounds of Nature

Procedure

1. Listen to the sounds of insects and other animals. Describe what you hear.

   Answers will vary, depending on the recordings

   available.

   _____

   _____

Materials

• recordings of insect sounds and sounds of other animals

2. What animals do you think you heard?

   Answers will vary, depending on the recordings available.

   Possible sounds include bear, cow, owl, buffalo, and so on.

3. For each animal you heard, identify the environment in which it lives.

   Answers will vary, depending on the recordings available.

   _____

   _____

Drawing Conclusions

1. How many different animals were you able to identify?

   Answers will vary.

   _____

2. How do insect sounds differ from the sounds of the other animals you heard?

   Insect sounds are usually high-pitched. Other animals, such as a

   cow, make sounds with a lower pitch.

© Macmillan/McGraw-Hill

Name_____ **Date**_____

Define Terms Based on Observations

What Makes Up a Forest Community?

You have learned that a community is all the living things in an ecosystem. Different ecosystems have different communities. For example, the pond community on pages B8 and B9 in your textbook includes bladderworts, frogs, algae, and dragonflies. What makes up a forest community? Look at the picture on this page. Use your observations to define a forest community.

Procedure

1. **Observe** Make a list of all the things you see in the picture of the forest.

   I see trees, rocks, grasses, flowers, a deer, a chipmunk, soil, birds, a lion, and
   a waterfall and stream.

2. Classify Which of the things on your list are living? Which are nonliving?

Living Things	Nonliving Things
Possible answers: trees, grasses, flowers, a deer, a chipmunk, birds, a lion	Rocks, water, and soil

Drawing Conclusions

Define Terms Using your list, explain what a forest community is.

Possible answers: A forest community includes nonliving things, such as soil, sunlight, water, and rocks. It includes plants and trees. It also includes animals, such as deer, birds, and chipmunks.

_____

_____

_____

_____

Where Does Food Come From?

Hypothesize People eat many different kinds of foods. Does more of the food you eat come from plants or animals? How might you investigate your ideas? Write a **Hypothesis:**

Possible hypothesis: Most of the foods that I eat come from plants.

_____

Procedure

1. **Observe** Look at the picture of the pizza on textbook page B15. What types of food do you see? Make a list.

   I see: tomatoes, onions, peppers,

   mushrooms, cheese, and pepperoni

2. **Classify** Next to each thing on your list, record whether the food comes from a plant or an animal. Write *P* for plant and *A* for animal.

   P: tomatoes, onions, peppers, and wheat for crust;

   A: cheese and pepperoni

   (Mushrooms are fungi, not plants.)

3. Look at your list of foods that come from animals. From which animal does each food come? What food does that animal eat?

   Possible answers: Cheese comes from a cow. The cow eats grasses, hay, feed,

   and grains. Pepperoni comes from a pig. A pig eats feed and grains.

   _____

Drawing Conclusions

1. If there were no plants, which foods would be left to make pizza? (**Hint:** Think about what animals eat to survive.)

   Possible answer: There would be no animals left to make a pizza.

   Animals eat plants, so they would also disappear.

2. **Infer** Do all foods come from plants? Explain your answer.

   Yes, all foods come from plants either directly or indirectly. Even if the

   food comes from an animal, the animal had to eat plants to live and grow.

3. Write down a food that you like to eat. List all of the ingredients in this food.

   Answers will vary.

4. **FURTHER INQUIRY** **Classify** Make a chart on a separate sheet of paper that shows where each ingredient in your favorite food comes from.

   Answers will vary depending on type of food chosen.

   _____

Inquiry

Think of your own questions that you might like to test.
Could you eat a diet based only on plants?

My Question Is:

Possible question: What would I eat if I were a vegetarian?

How I Can Test It:

Possible answer: I can ask a person who is a vegetarian what he or

she eats. I can look at recipes in a vegetarian cookbook or magazine.

My Results Are:

Answers will vary. Possible answer: Vegetarians eat fruits,

vegetables, soy products, grains, nuts, and beans.

What's in Food?

Procedure

Materials

- labels of various prepared foods

1. Look at the label of a prepared food. Foods such as cereal, cookies, and pasta are found in boxes. Vegetables and sauces are found in cans.

2. What is on the front of the can or box?

   Usually, the front of the package shows what the product inside looks like.

3. What do you think is in the package?

   Students will likely expect that the contents will look just like the label.

4. Look at the label that lists the ingredients. Does the list match your prediction? Explain.

   No, the label will show all the various ingredients that are used in the food.

Drawing Conclusions

1. Was there anything in the ingredients list that you did not expect to see? Explain.

   Answers will vary, but may include such items as preservatives,

   coloring agents, and salt.

2. Was there anything that you expected to see in the ingredients list that you did not see? Explain.

   Answers will vary, but may include things shown in the photograph

   as "serving suggestions" that are not in the product.

QUICK LAB
FOR SCHOOL OR HOME
Lesson 2

Decomposers

Hypothesize What will happen to bread and apples if they are left out for one week? Write a **Hypothesis:**

Possible hypothesis: The color will change and organisms will

be growing on the bread and apples.

Materials

- **1 self-sealing plastic bag**
- **apple pieces**

Procedure

BE CAREFUL! Don't open the sealed bag.

1. Put some apple pieces in a plastic bag. Seal the bag.

2. **Observe** Leave the apples in the bag for one week. Observe the apples every day. Record your observation.

   Answers will vary.

3. What happened to the pieces of apple?

   The apple will be covered with fuzzy material, possibly green or black in

   color.

©Macmillan/McGraw-Hill

Drawing Conclusions

4. What does this activity tell you about decomposers?

Possible answers: They are organisms growing on the apple. They are breaking down the apple. They have different colors and appearances.

5. Infer What would happen if there were no decomposers?

Earth would be covered by dead plant and animal material.

6. Going Further Think of your own questions that you might like to test. What other materials will decomposers break down?

My Question Is:

Possible question: Will decomposers break down vegetables?

How I Can Test It:

Possible answer: I can repeat the experiment using vegetables, such as potatoes.

My Results Are:

Possible answer: Decomposers break down vegetables.

How Do Living Things Meet Their Needs?

Hypothesize Pets and houseplants have people to take care of them. How do plants and animals in nature get what they need to live and grow? How might you test your ideas? Write a **Hypothesis:**

Possible hypothesis: Plants get water, air, and sunlight.

Animals get food from plants and catch other animals as prey.

Materials

- gravel
- guppy or goldfish
- small water plants
- 2-L plastic drink bottle
- bottom of another drink bottle with holes
- fish food

Procedure

BE CAREFUL! Handle animals carefully. Measure materials carefully.

1. **Make a Model** Put a 3–cm layer of gravel into the plastic drink bottle. Fill the bottle three-quarters full of water. Anchor the plants in the gravel.

2. Cover the bottle with the bottom of another bottle. Do not place it in direct sunlight.

3. After two days, gently place the fish into the bottle. Add a few flakes of fish food.

4. **Observe** Look at your ecosystem every day for two weeks. Feed the fish twice each week. Record your observations on a separate sheet of paper.

Drawing Conclusions

1. What did the fish need to survive? What did the plants need to survive?

Possible answers: The fish needed food, water, air, sunlight, and plants to survive. The plants needed water, air, and sunlight to make food to survive.

_____

2. What might happen if the plant was not part of the ecosystem?

Possible answer: The fish might die because it needs the oxygen that the
plant produces.

3. FURTHER INQUIRY Experiment How do frogs meet their needs?
Predict what kind of ecosystem you would need to build to find out.
How do you know?

Frogs will probably need a wet terrarium that provides dry land and water,
and a supply of insects or another food. Frogs need food, water,
air, and sunlight to survive.

Inquiry

Think of your own questions that you might like to test. What kind of
food do fish eat?

My Question Is:

Possible question: What is the fish food made of?

How I Can Test It:

Possible answer: I can read the label on the container of fish food.

My Results Are:

Possible answer: Most fish food contains dried, chopped shrimp, brine shrimp, or
ant pupae. Others have dried vegetables added.

Life Cycle

Procedure

1. Observe an aquarium or the ecosystem that you set up in the Explore Activity. List the living things in your ecosystem.

   fish and water plant

2. Draw your ecosystem. Add arrows to the drawing to show the exchange of oxygen and carbon dioxide. One arrow should point from the oxygen producer to the oxygen user. Another arrow should point from the carbon dioxide producer to the carbon dioxide user. Remember to label the arrows.

   The drawing should include this cycle; fish gives off carbon dioxide; plants use carbon dioxide; plants give off oxygen; fish uses oxygen

Materials

- gravel

- guppy or goldfish

- small water plants

- 2-L plastic drink bottle

- bottom of another drink bottle

- fish food

Drawing Conclusions

1. In your ecosystem, which living thing produces oxygen?

   plants

2. In your ecosystem, which living thing produces carbon dioxide?

   fish

Traveling Seeds

Hypothesize Animals with fur often help plants spread their seeds. How might they do this? Write a **Hypothesis:**

Possible hypothesis: Seeds that get stuck on an animal's fur

may get deposited in a different area.

Materials

- seeds
- fake fur

Procedure

1. **Predict** What will happen when you toss seeds onto a piece of fake fur? Record your prediction.

   Some of the seeds will stick to the fur.

2. **Experiment** Test your prediction. Have your partner hold up the fur. Toss different seeds at it. Record the results.

   Burrs and seeds with hooks should stick to the fur.

© Macmillan/McGraw-Hill

Drawing Conclusions

3. Identify Which of the seeds stuck to the fur? Were your predictions correct? Write your answer.

Burrs and seeds with hooks stuck to the fur.

_____

_____

_____

4. Going Further Think of your own questions that you might like to test. What animal behaviors cause them to have seeds stuck to their fur?

My Question Is:

Possible question: Do animals pick up seeds by walking beside trees or by

rolling around on the ground?

How I Can Test It:

Possible answer: I can drop seeds from above onto the fur and roll the fur

onto a pile of seeds.

My Results Are:

Possible answer: Both behaviors cause animals to have seeds stuck

to their fur.

How Much Room Do Plants Need?

Hypothesize You know that space is one of the needs of living things. When there are too many people in one place, it gets uncomfortable! What happens when there are too many plants in one place? Does the amount of space available affect the way plants grow? Write a **Hypothesis:**

Possible hypothesis: When there are too many plants, some

cannot grow. They will crowd each other out.

Materials

- soil
- bean seeds
- 4 milk cartons
- measuring cup
- water
- masking tape
- marker

Procedure

1. Cut the tops from the milk cartons. Use the masking tape and a marker to label the cartons A to D. Use the measuring cup to fill each carton with the same amount of soil.

2. **Use Variables** Plant 3 bean seeds in carton A. Plant 6 bean seeds in carton B. Plant 12 bean seeds in carton C and 24 bean seeds in carton D.

3. **Predict** What do you think each carton will look like in 14 days? Record your predictions on a separate sheet of paper.

4. **Experiment** Place the cartons in a well-lighted area. Water the plants every two days. Use the same amount of water for each carton. Record any changes you observe in the plants.

Drawing Conclusions

1. How do the plants in carton D compare to the plants in the other cartons?

   Possible answer: The plants in carton D look spindly and are light green.

2. What are the plants competing for?

Possible answer: They are competing for space, nutrients in soil, water, and sunlight.

3. Repeat this activity. Compare your results. What happened?

The results should be similar.

4. **FURTHER INQUIRY** **Infer** How do plants in your neighborhood compete for what they need to grow?

Answers will vary. Possible answer: Small trees shaded by a larger tree compete for limited space that receives sunlight. Plants may also compete for water in dry periods.

Inquiry

Think of your own questions that you might like to test using the materials from this activity. What would happen if these plants competed for only one of the things that they need to live?

My Question Is:

Possible question: How would the plants in each carton compare if they competed only for water?

How I Can Test It:

Possible answer: I can plant 6 seeds in each carton. I will water the plants in carton A every 2 days, plants in carton B every 4 days, plants in carton C every week, and plants in carton D every 10 days.

My Results Are:

Possible answer: The plants in carton A grow quicker than those in carton B. Plants in cartons C and D do not grow.

© Macmillan/McGraw-Hill

Competition for Space

Procedure

Materials

• plants and trees in a yard, park, forest, or field

1. Look at an area where plants and trees are growing naturally.

2. Observe how the plants are spaced and how large they are. Record your observations.

   Answers will vary.

   _____

   _____

3. Do any of the plants grow in the shade of larger plants? If so, describe them.

   It is likely that some plants grow in the shade, but more grow in

   the sunny areas.

   _____

Drawing Conclusions

1. Which kinds of plants grow in shaded areas?

   Answers will vary depending on the area visited. In a forested

   area, ferns grow in the shade.

2. Compare the amount of space and sunlight that different plants need.

   Answers will vary depending on plants observed. Students should

   recognize that plants that grow in the shade of larger plants need

   less sunlight than the larger plants, and that smaller plants need

   less space than larger plants.

Name_____ Date_____

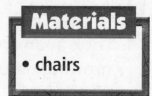

FOR SCHOOL OR HOME
Lesson 4

Musical Chairs

Hypothesize How does changing the number of chairs affect the game musical chairs? Write a **Hypothesis:**

Possible hypothesis: People will compete for a different

number of chairs.

Materials

• chairs

Procedure

1. Play a game of musical chairs.

2. **Experiment** Change the number of chairs you play with. How does this affect the game? Record your observations.

   Answers will vary depending on whether chairs are added or taken away.

Drawing Conclusions

3. What do the players compete for in musical chairs?

   A chair to sit on.

4. **Communicate** How is the competition in the game like competition in a real ecosystem?

   Organisms compete for a limited amount of what they need.

5. **Going Further** Think of your own questions that you might like to test. How do people win the competition for chairs?

My Question Is:

Possible question: What things might help someone win a game of musical chairs?

How I Can Test It:

Possible answer: I can observe a game of musical chairs and see what makes the winners win.

My Results Are:

Possible answer: Luck, alertness, and speed help someone win a game of musical chairs.

How Does the Shape of a Bird's Beak Affect What It Eats?

Hypothesize All birds have beaks, but different kinds of birds have different kinds of beaks. How does a bird's beak help it eat the foods it needs? Write a **Hypothesis:**

Possible hypothesis: Different beak shapes are suited to different kinds of food.

Procedure: Design Your Own

1. **Predict** How does the shape of a bird's beak affect what it eats? Record your predictions on a separate sheet of paper.

2. **Make a Model** Look at the materials given to you. How will you use them? Record your plan.

   Answers will vary. Possible answer: I will use the chopsticks, spoon, and clothespin to crack open and pick up food, and the drinking straw to drink liquids.

3. Record your data in the chart below.

4. Follow your plan. Be sure to record all your observations.

Type of Beak	Type of Food	Observations
chopsticks	worm	chopsticks able to pick up worm that is hard to grasp
spoon	rice, water	spoon able to scoop up rice, water
clothespin	worm, peanut	clothespin able to crack peanut
drinking straw	water	straw pulls up water

Materials

- chopsticks
- spoon
- clothespin
- drinking straw
- rubber worm
- peanut in shell
- rice
- water in paper cup

© Macmillan/McGraw-Hill

Drawing Conclusions

1. Share your chart with your classmates. How are your results similar? How are they different? Why is it important to compare your results with those of your classmates?

   Charts will be similar. Some students may be more adept at using tools.

2. Explain why different tools are better suited to different jobs.

   Some tools can pick up materials better than others because of

   their shape.

3. **Infer** How does the shape of a bird's beak help it to eat the foods it needs? How do you know?

   The shape of the beak is important because some birds crack shells or

   hard nuts, others pick up tiny seeds, still others grasp moving prey.

4. **FURTHER INQUIRY** **Experiment** Are different teeth better for eating different foods? How would you test your ideas?

   Yes. Possible answer: Try grinding leaves with the smooth faces of rocks

   (as models of molars) versus corners of rocks (as models of incisors).

Inquiry

Think of your own questions that you might like to test. Which tool is easiest to use to feed food to another person?

My Question Is:

Possible question: Which tool can I eat more rice with?

How I Can Test It:

Possible answer: I can use each tool and see which one works best.

My Results Are:

Possible answer: When I use the spoon, I can eat more rice.

Comparing Beaks

Procedure

Materials

• reference books

1. Choose a bird to look up in an encyclopedia or nature book. Find a picture of the bird.

2. Make a large drawing of the bird's beak in the space below.

3. Find other students whose drawings are similar to yours. What characteristics do all the beaks share?

    Beaks should be similar in length and shape.
    _____
    _____

4. Discuss with your group the kind of food that would be eaten by a bird with this kind of beak.

Drawing Conclusions

1. How would you describe the shape of the beak that you drew?

    Answers will vary depending on bird.
    _____
    _____

2. What kind of food would this bird eat? Explain your answer.

    Answers will vary depending on bird. Answers should reflect an understanding
    of the relationship between beak shape and what food the bird eats.
    _____

©Macmillan/McGraw-Hill

Observe

Design an Animal

You know that camouflage is one way animals keep safe. In this activity you will observe an area of your classroom. When you observe something, you use one or more of your senses to learn about the objects. You will use your observations of your classroom to help you design an animal that could hide in that environment.

Materials

• construction paper

• crayons

• cotton balls

• yarn

• scissors

• tape

Procedure

BE CAREFUL! Be careful when using scissors.

1. **Observe** Select an area to observe. This area is the environment for the organism that you will design. What do you notice about the area? What colors do you see? What textures do you feel? Record your observations.

   Answers will vary depending upon the area. Answers will include different colors and textures.

2. Create a plan with a classmate. Make a list of features that would help an organism hide in this environment.

   Answers will vary depending upon features in the area. Features may include color and size.

© Macmillan/McGraw-Hill

3. Use the materials given to you to create a plant or an animal that will blend into its surroundings. Put your plant or animal into its environment.

Drawing Conclusions

1. Describe the characteristics of the organism that you made. Explain why you included each one.

Characteristics will vary depending on the environment and how the

organism will best blend in with it.

_____

_____

_____

2. **Infer** Some animals can change the color of their body covering. Why might they do this?

Answers will vary. Possible answer: They might change their color

if another organism was trying to catch them. This would help

them escape.

_____

_____

What Happens When Ecosystems Change?

Hypothesize A big storm or volcanic eruption can cause a lot of change in a short amount of time. How do changes like these affect the living things in a particular area? How might you use a model to investigate your ideas? Write a **Hypothesis**:

Possible hypothesis: Some living things might have

trouble surviving.

Materials

• 3 predator cards: red hawk, blue owl, green snake

• 12 prey cards: 4 red, 4 blue, 4 green

Procedure

1. Make the 3 predator and 12 prey cards listed in the Materials. Give each player one predator card. Stack the prey cards in the center of the table.

2. Take turns drawing a prey card. Keep only the prey cards that match the color of your predator card. Return all others. Play until one predator gets all four matching prey cards.

3. **Experiment** Add a card that says "fire" to the prey cards. Play the game again. Any predator who draws the fire card must leave the game. Return the fire card to the deck. Continue to play until a predator gets all four prey cards or all players are out.

Drawing Conclusions

1. What happened each time you played the game?

All of the prey cards from one predator were gone; some of the other

prey cards were left. The second time, as the predators drop out when

they get the fire card, their prey cards stay on the pile.

Explore
Activity
Lesson 6

2. The fire card represented an ecosystem change.
   What effect did it have?

   It eliminated predators from the ecosystem and their prey increased.

   _____

3. **Infer** What may happen when an ecosystem changes?

   Possible answer: The balance of predators and prey can change.

   Some habitats and foods can disappear, so organisms move or die.

4. FURTHER INQUIRY **Predict** What might happen if you changed the
   number of prey cards? Try it.

   Possible answer: More prey cards: it would take longer for the predators to

   be removed from play. Fewer prey cards: predators would be removed faster.

Inquiry

Think of your own questions that you might like to test using the cards.
What would happen if you added another card to the game?

My Question Is:

Possible question: What would happen if I added a card that says "new habitat" to

the deck? Any predator who draws the new habitat card would get a second turn.

How I Can Test It:

Possible answer: I can play the game using the new habitat card.

My Results Are:

Possible answer: Whichever player draws the new habitat card has a

better chance of getting the 4 matching prey cards.

© Macmillan/McGraw-Hill

Create an Ecosystem

Procedure

Materials

• blank cards

1. Work in a group to create a set of cards that show predators, prey, foods, and habitats in an ecosystem.

2. List the cards your group made.

   Answers will vary.

   _____

3. As a group, create a game in which the cards are organized as an ecosystem. In your game, making a change in a card should change the ecosystem. List the rules of your game.

   Games should be similar to the game played in the Explore activity.

   _____

   _____

   _____

   _____

Drawing Conclusions

1. Did you have to make extra cards as you developed the game? Why or why not?

   As students develop the game, they may discover that they are

   missing some key elements in their ecosystem.

2. Did your game show how the ecosystem changed when you changed a card?

   Answers will vary depending on the rules.

Crowd Control

Hypothesize What happens when the same number of organisms move into a smaller habitat? Write a **Hypothesis:**

Possible hypothesis: Some organisms cannot get the food or
water they need to survive.

Materials

- 20 paper clips
- small box
- small book

Procedure

1. Toss 20 paper clips in a small box. Remove any two that touch each other.

2. Gather the paper clips that are left in the box. Toss them again and remove any two that touch. Repeat until there are no clips left. Count how many tosses you made.

   Answers will vary.

   _____

   _____

3. Repeat steps 1 and 2. This time put a book into the box so there is less room for the clips to move in. Record the number of tosses you made.

   Answers will vary.

   _____

©Macmillan/McGraw-Hill

Drawing Conclusions

4. **Infer** When organisms are crowded together, how do their chances of survival change?

When organisms are crowded, individuals cannot get access to food,

water, or space. Their chances of survival become low.

_____

5. **Going Further** Think about your own questions that you might like to test. What happens to the organisms if a new predator lives in the smaller habitat?

My Question Is:

Possible question: How are the organisms affected if an equal-sized

population of predators lives in the new habitat?

How I Can Test It:

Possible answer: I can repeat the experiment, this time tossing in an equal

number of paper clips of another color or size to represent the predator.

I will remove all the "prey" paper clips that are touched by a "predator"

paper clip.

My Results Are:

Possible answer: The prey organisms have a much lower chance of surviving.

_____

How Are Rocks Alike and Different?

Hypothesize What makes up rocks? Are all rocks alike? How might you test your ideas?

Write a **Hypothesis:**

Possible hypothesis: Rocks are made up of bits of solids. They are not all alike.

Materials

- several different rocks
- hand lens

Procedure

1. Touch each rock. Describe how each rock feels.

   Answers will vary depending on rocks. Most rocks will feel hard.

2. **Observe** Carefully look at each rock. Write about any lines or patterns you see.

   Answers will vary depending on rocks.

3. **Observe** Look at each rock through the hand lens. Write or draw any new things you see.

   Students may see more details of the rocks, such as lines or differences in color.

Drawing Conclusions

1. Did any rocks feel the same? Did any rocks have similar lines or patterns?

   Some textures may be similar. Lines and patterns in the rocks will probably vary considerably.

©Macmillan/McGraw-Hill

2. Describe how the rocks are alike. Describe how they are different.

Possible answer: All the rocks contain shiny bits.

3. **Infer** Do you think the rocks are made of one material or many materials? Explain.

Differences in color, shape, hardness, and shine show that the rocks are made of more than one material.

4. FURTHER INQUIRY **Classify** How might you classify the rocks into two or more groups? What physical properties of the rocks will be helpful? Try it to test your idea.

Physical properties such as hardness, color, shape, size, shine, texture, and number of materials making up the rock are all means of grouping rocks.

Inquiry

Think of your own questions that you might like to test. How else are rocks alike or different?

My Question Is:

Possible answer: Are rocks alike or different in weight?

How I Can Test It:

Possible answer: I can compare the weight of rocks that are about the same size by holding them in my hand.

My Results Are:

Answers will vary depending on rocks tested.

More Rocks

Procedure

1. Work in groups to investigate rocks.

2. First, examine all of the rocks that you have. Discuss as a group what characteristics of the rocks you will look at.

3. List the characteristics your group will investigate.

   Possible answers: hardness, color, shape, shine, texture,

   and makeup

   _____

4. Draw the rocks in the space below. Below each drawing, write the characteristics of the rock. Use extra paper if you need more room.

Materials

• rocks brought in from home

• hand lens

Drawing Conclusions

1. How are the rocks you examined alike?

   Results will depend on the variety of rocks examined.

   _____

2. How are the rocks you examined different?

   Results will depend on the variety of rocks examined.

   _____

©Macmillan/McGraw-Hill

Mineral Scratch Test

Hypothesize Which of these minerals do you think is the hardest?

Write a **Hypothesis:**

Possible hypothesis: Quartz is the hardest.

Materials

- three minerals
- penny
- *paper clip*

Procedure

1. Your teacher will give you three minerals. Draw each mineral in a column on a piece of paper.

2. **Predict** Which mineral will be the easiest to scratch? Which will be the most difficult? Write your predictions in a second column next to your drawings.

   Predictions will vary.

3. **Observe** Test your predictions. Scratch each mineral with your fingernail, a penny, *and a paper clip* Record your observations in a third column.

   Answers will vary.

Drawing Conclusions

4. **Interpret Data** Number the minerals you tested in order of hardness, from hardest to softest. Make a fourth column to place your numbers.

   Answers will vary.

© Macmillan/McGraw-Hill

Explore Activity
Lesson 2

What Is in Soil?

Hypothesize You know that soil is important for growing plants. What is in soil? How might you test your ideas?

Write a **Hypothesis:**

Possible hypothesis: Soil is made up of bits of leaves, plants, _____

and rocks. _____

Materials

- small amount of soil
- piece of white paper
- hand lens

Procedure

1. Spread the soil on the piece of paper.

2. **Observe** Look at the soil closely. What do you see? Are there different colors? Are there pieces of different sizes?

   Possible answer: The soil includes different sizes and colors of rock and

   plant particles.

3. **Observe** Touch the soil. How does it feel? Smell the soil. How does it smell? Record your observations. Be sure to wash your hands after you touch the soil.

   Possible answer: The soil smells musty and feels sometimes gritty and

   sometimes soft. It has a dark brown color.

4. Use a hand lens to look at the soil. What can you see now? Record your observations.

   Possible answer: The soil includes tiny grains of sand and clay and bits

   of leaves.

© Macmillan/McGraw-Hill

● **Drawing Conclusions**

1. Describe the soil. Tell how it looks, smells, and feels.

   Students may describe small and larger bits of rock and sand. It may feel

   rough or slippery.

2. **Infer** What different materials make up the soil?

   Students may be surprised at the number of different types of particles in

   the soil.

3. **FURTHER INQUIRY** **Form a Hypothesis** Form a hypothesis that explains how soil forms. Test your hypothesis. What did you find out?

   Students may say the particles got into the soil from rocks, dead plants, or

   pieces of bark from trees.

Inquiry

● Think of your own questions that you might like to test. How is soil different in different places?

My Question Is:

Possible answer: How is soil from two different places different?

How I Can Test It:

Possible answer: I can collect, observe, and compare soil from two

different places.

My Results Are:

Possible answer: Soil from different places contains different kinds

of particles.

Alternative Explore

Lesson 2

Comparing Soils

Procedure

Materials

- soil from home
- piece of white paper
- hand lens

1. Bring in a small amount of soil from home.

2. On a piece of white paper, write where the sample came from.

3. Spread out your soil sample on the paper.

4. Tour your classroom, looking at five different soil samples. Notice the color of the soil, how large the particles are, and how the soil feels when you touch it.

5. Record your observations.

Answers will vary depending on the soil samples.

_____

_____

_____

_____

Drawing Conclusions

1. How were the soil samples you looked at similar?

Answers will vary, depending on the soil samples. Possible answers: Each

sample was the same color.

2. How were they different?

Answers will vary, depending on the soil samples. Possible answers: Some of

the samples had different textures.

© Macmillan/McGraw-Hill

Measure

How Much Water Can Soil Hold?

In this activity, you will measure and compare the amounts of water held by two different soils.

Procedure

1. **Measure** Fill the measuring cup with 250 mL of potting soil. Put the soil into a paper cup with holes in the bottom. Pack the soil firmly. Fill the measuring cup with 100 mL of water.

2. **Experiment** Hold the cup of potting soil over an empty paper cup without holes. Have a partner slowly pour the water into the soil. Let the water run through the soil for two minutes.

3. **Measure** Pour the water you collected into the measuring cup. Record the volume in a chart.

   Answers will vary depending on the soil sample used.

   _____

4. **Experiment** Repeat steps 1–3 using sandy soil. Record the volume.

   Answers will vary depending on the soil sample used.

   _____

Materials

- 4 paper cups, 2 with holes in the bottom
- measuring cup
- water
- potting soil
- sandy soil
- watch or clock
- calculator (optional)

© Macmillan/McGraw-Hill

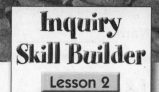

Drawing Conclusions

1. **Infer** Which soil held more water? How do you know?

   The potting soil held more water. Students know because there was less

   water in the measuring cup, so more stayed in the soil.

2. Which kind of soil would be better for a garden? Which would be better for a soccer field?

   The potting soil would be better for a garden because it would hold more

   water. The sandy soil would be better for a soccer field because it would

   be drier.

3. **Interpret Data** Repeat this activity and record the data in a chart. Compare your results. Compare your findings with a classmate's. What did you find out? Summarize your results.

   The results should be similar when repeated. Potting soil holds more water

   than sandy soil.

How Are Fossils Formed?

Hypothesize How can you make a model to show how fossils are formed?

Write a **Hypothesis:**

Students will probably describe a process, such as squeezing

or burying some object.

Materials

- large plastic spoon
- clear glue
- 2 slices of carrot
- paper towel

Procedure

1. Squeeze a small amount of glue into the spoon. Let the glue set for a few hours.

2. Place one slice of carrot on top of the glue. Slowly add more glue until the carrot slice is completely covered. Place the spoon on a paper towel. Put the other slice of carrot next to the spoon.

3. Compare the glue and carrot to fossil insects in amber.

   Students should notice that the carrot and insects can be seen through

   the glue and amber.

   _____

4. **Observe** Compare the carrot slices. Describe their color and appearance.

   Have students brainstorm words that describe the carrots' appearance and

   could be used to record their observations.

   _____

©Macmillan/McGraw-Hill

Drawing Conclusions

1. **How did the glue change the carrot slice?**

   The glue covered the carrot slice but otherwise did not change it. Only the

   outer part of the carrot has a glue coat.

2. **Predict** Over time, will the carrot slice in the glue change more than the other carrot slice? Why?

   No, the carrot slice in the glue should change much less than the uncovered

   carrot slice. The glued slice is protected from air, water, and other forces

   of nature.

3. **FURTHER INQUIRY** **Experiment** With a team member, design and conduct an experiment to test your prediction.

   Possible answer: After a few days of leaving both carrots in a safe, dry place,

   the glued carrot slice should remain the same while the other carrot slice

   will have changed color or texture slightly.

Inquiry

Think of your own questions that you might like to test. How do the tracks of animals appear as fossils?

My Question Is:

Possible answer: How do animal tracks get to be fossils?

How I Can Test It:

Possible answer: Make a mold using clay. Use objects to make impressions.

My Results Are:

Impressions that look like fossils were imprinted in the clay.

© Macmillan/McGraw-Hill

Fossil Stories

Procedure

1. Work in small groups.

2. Discuss how fossils give clues about past life on Earth.

3. Carefully observe the small objects.

4. Decide how to create a "fossil story" about the past. Talk about which small objects to use and in which order to use them.

5. Press the objects into the slab of clay. Make clear imprints.

6. Now write what your "fossil story" tells about the past below.

   Accounts should describe living things that lived on Earth in the distant past.

   _____

   _____

   _____

   _____

   _____

Drawing Conclusions

1. How is your "fossil story" similar to real fossils?

   Both the "fossil story" and real fossils give clues about happenings. Neither uses words.

   _____

   _____

2. How does your "fossil story" differ from real fossils?

   The "fossil story" is fiction based on happenings in the present. Fossils are clues to actual happenings in the past.

   _____

©Macmillan/McGraw-Hill

QUICK LAB

FOR SCHOOL OR HOME

Lesson 3

Imprint Clues

Hypothesize How can you identify what object made an imprint?

Write a **Hypothesis:**

The object has the same outer shape as the imprint.

Materials

- modeling clay
- small objects (coins, math cubes, and so on)

Procedure

1. Gather three small objects. Form some modeling clay into a thick, flat layer.

2. **Make a Model** Press an object into the clay. It should make an imprint. Carefully remove the object.

3. Repeat step 2 with two other objects.

Drawing Conclusions

4. **Infer** Exchange imprint models with a classmate. Try to figure out which objects were used.

   Answers will vary.

5. Share your ideas with the class.

   Answers will vary.

Where Do Lakes Form?

Hypothesize How can you make a model to show where lakes are formed?

Write a **Hypothesis:**

Students may suggest filling a hole in a pot of soil or sand.
_____

_____

Materials

- clear-plastic box

- modeling clay

- water

Procedure

1. **Make a Model** Place the clay in the clear-plastic box. Mold it into different landforms. Make mountains, hills, and valleys. Clay should cover most of the bottom of the box.

2. **Predict** You have modeled land without water. If you added water, where would lakes form?

   Students should predict that lakes will form in the lowest areas.
   _____

   _____

3. **Observe** Gently pour water into the box. Stop when you see one or more small lakes forming. Draw a diagram of the land with water. Add more water to the model.

   Students will observe that lakes will form in the lowest areas.
   _____

   _____

   _____

Drawing Conclusions

1. Where did lakes form in your model?

   Lakes formed in the lowest areas.

2. Compare your model with real land and water. How are they alike? How are they different?

   Both have high areas and low areas. However, the model has very thick "soil"

   that does not absorb water, has no plants or trees, and has no precipitation.

3. **Infer** Could lakes ever form where there are mountains? Explain.

   Students should infer that lakes could form in mountains if the land around

   them was high enough to prevent the water from flowing to lower levels.

4. **FURTHER INQUIRY** Rain has been falling for many days, and Lake Elmo is rising. What do you need to know to predict where the water will go? Compare your ideas with your classmates'.

   The location of the lowest point on Lake Elmo's shore; when the water gets

   high enough, it will pour out of the lake at that point.

Inquiry

Think of your own questions that you might like to test. How do you think rivers and streams are formed?

My Question Is:

Possible question: Can rivers and streams be formed by rainfall coming off

a mountain?

How I Can Test It:

Possible answer: Make a model of a mountain using dirt or sand. Pour some water

over the top of the "mountain."

My Results Are:

Possible answer: A "river" is dug into the dirt by the running water.

© Macmillan/McGraw-Hill

**Alternative
Explore**

Lesson 4

Escaping Water

Procedure

1. Work in pairs. Carefully observe the paper cup. Notice where the slit is cut in the cup.

2. Use the marker to make a mark on the cup showing the highest level of water it will hold.

3. Now fill your cup at the sink.

4. Did you mark the correct spot? Where is the correct spot located?

   The correct spot is located right below the slit.
   _____

5. What happens if the spot you marked was too high?

   The water will escape through the slit.
   _____

6. What happens if the spot you marked was too low?

   No water will escape through the slit.
   _____

Materials
• paper cup with slit

Drawing Conclusions

1. Explain how the cup acts like land and the water inside the cup acts like a lake.

   The land around a lake is high enough to keep the water from pouring out.
   _____

2. At which point would the water in the lake pour out if it got high enough?

   The water would flow out of the lake at the lowest point on the lake's shore.
   _____

© Macmillan/McGraw-Hill

Wasting Water

How Much Water Do You Use?

Activity	Normal Use
Showering	95 liters
Bathing	150 liters
Brushing teeth	18 liters
Washing hands	8 liters
Dishwasher	60 liters
Washing clothes	220 liters

Materials
- calculator (optional)

Procedure

1. **Form a Hypothesis** How much water do you think you use in a day? Record your prediction.

   Answers will vary.

2. Write down each daily activity in which you use water. Use the back of this sheet or separate paper.

3. Use the chart to see how much water each activity uses.

4. **Use Numbers** Add the number of liters of water used for each activity. Calculate the amount of water used in a day.

   Answers will vary.

Drawing Conclusions

5. Compare your results with the prediction. How can you use less water?

   To save water, students might suggest taking a shower instead of a bath, do not run water while brushing or washing hands.

© Macmillan/McGraw-Hill

How Does Mining Affect the Land?

Hypothesize Some natural resources, such as diamonds and metals, are hard to find. What effect do you think mining these resources might have on Earth's land? How might you use a model to test your ideas?

Write a **Hypothesis:**

Possible hypothesis: Mining may disturb the land.

_____

_____

Materials

• chocolate chip cookie

• 4 toothpicks

• paper towel

Procedure

1. **Observe** Place the cookie on the paper towel. Draw the cookie, and label its parts. The chips represent resources. The cookie represents the land.

2. **Model** Use toothpicks to remove the chocolate chips. Try not to damage the cookie. Mine all the resources from the land.

3. **Observe** Draw the cookie again.

Drawing Conclusions

1. How did mining change the cookie?

   Students' drawings should include labels for "resource" and "land." The

   cookie looks broken up, with holes where the chips were.

   _____

2. If you needed more resources than you found in the land, how could you get them?

You would need to locate them in another place.

3. Infer What are some problems people face when they mine resources from Earth?

People might have the problem of breaking up Earth to mine, or otherwise harming the land.

4. **FURTHER INQUIRY** **Infer** How can damage to mining areas be repaired? How do you know? Test your ideas on your cookie and report your results.

Students may say damage could be repaired through filling up the holes with other land, and covering over the cracks with land. They may have seen roads or areas that were repaved or repaired.

Inquiry

Think of your own questions that you might like to test. How much harder is it to mine underneath the surface of Earth than on its surface?

My Question Is:

Possible question: What can go wrong when mining below Earth's surface?

How I Can Test It:

Possible answer: I can mine by digging a hole in soil.

My Results Are:

Possible answer: Soil from the sides of the hole falls down as I dig.

Mining Methods

Procedure

BE CAREFUL! Do not taste the liquid.

1. One method of mining is to dissolve minerals and then separate them. In this activity you will separate a mixture of sand and sugar.

2. In a small container, mix some sand and some sugar.

3. Add water to the mixture and stir it.

4. Allow the mixture to settle. Then pour off the liquid into a second container.

5. If this liquid is cloudy, allow it to settle for a few minutes. Then pour some of the liquid into a shallow plate and leave it in a warm place.

6. When the liquid has dried up, observe the plate.

Materials

- sugar
- sand
- 2 small containers
- water
- plastic spoon
- shallow plate

Drawing Conclusions

1. What happened to the mixture when you added water?

   Some of the mixture dissolved.
   _____

2. When you poured some of the liquid into the second container, what was left in the first container?

   Sand and some of the liquid.
   _____

3. What was left in the plate after the water dried up?

   Sugar
   _____

Cleaning Water

Hypothesize Can you clean water by letting it flow through rocks?

Write a **Hypothesis:**

Possible hypothesis: Water is cleaned as it flows

through rocks.

Procedure **BE CAREFUL!** Wear goggles.

1. **Model** Place a funnel inside the bottom half of a plastic bottle. Put a layer of gravel in the funnel, and cover it with a layer of sand.

2. Mix a cup of water with a little soil and some crushed leaves. Slowly pour the mixture into the funnel.

Drawing Conclusions

3. **Observe** Draw the mixture in the space below. Describe how the mixture changed as it went through the funnel.

The water is clean. The soil is trapped in the sand and gravel.

Materials

- plastic funnel
- bottom half of plastic bottle
- gravel
- sand
- measuring cup
- water
- spoonful of soil
- dead leaves
- cup
- safety goggles

4. How does Earth clean water? Make a diagram on a separate piece of paper.

Earth cleans water as it soaks through soil and rock layers. Soil and rocks trap

particles in the water, allowing clean water to trickle through.

© Macmillan/McGraw-Hill

How Do the Features of Earth's Surface Compare?

Procedure

1. **Observe** Study the photos in your science book on page C53. How are the pictures alike? How are they different? Discuss these questions with a partner.

2. **Classify** Sort the pictures into two groups. Describe how you sorted them.

   tall /short; bumpy/flat; water/land

3. **Classify** Repeat step 2. This time try to sort the pictures into three groups.

Drawing Conclusions

1. What categories did you sort the pictures into?

   The mountain, the canyon, and the hills are the "bumpiest" places, while the others are flatter. The bay and valley are the wettest.

2. **Infer** For each picture, list some living things that could live in the place shown.

   Students should distinguish between land animals and plants and those in water.

3. **FURTHER INQUIRY** **Predict** For each picture, predict how the land might change during a year. How might it change after many years?

   During a year, snow and rain could fall on each place; each place could become warmer or colder. Over a long period, the mountains might get flatter; the bay could get larger or smaller; the prairie and valley might stay the same for a long time.

©Macmillan/McGraw-Hill

Comparing Landforms

Procedure

Materials

- photographs of landforms on page C53

1. Look at the photographs of different landforms.

2. Which landforms are high?

   mountain, hills

3. Which ones are wide?

   canyon, valley

4. Which landforms are deep?

   canyon

5. Name which ones are flat.

   prairie, bay

6. Which landforms are wet?

   bay

Drawing Conclusions

What are some other words you can use to describe landforms?

Possible answers: Dry, tropical, grassy, shady, icy, salty.

© Macmillan/McGraw-Hill

How Do Rocks Change?

Hypothesize Chalk is a kind of rock made up of the mineral calcite. How do you think the chalk got its shape? What are some ways you could change its shape? How might you test your ideas?

Write a **Hypothesis:**

Possible hypothesis: The chalk got its shape by being worn

down over time. Its shape could be changed by writing with it.

_____

Materials

• 3 pieces of chalk, different colors

• sandpaper

Procedure

1. **Observe** Look at the pieces of chalk and the sandpaper. Write down what they look and feel like.

   Possible answer: Chalk looks white, feels smooth and powdery.

   Sandpaper feels rough, looks like it is made of sand grains.

   _____

2. **Predict** What do you think will happen when you draw with the chalk on the sandpaper? Record your prediction.

   Possible answer: The chalk will leave a white mark on the sandpaper.

   _____

3. **Experiment** Use the chalk to write or draw on the sandpaper.

4. **Observe** Look at how the chalk and the sandpaper changed each other. Record your observations.

   Chalk is rough where it touched sandpaper. Parts of sandpaper are covered

   with white chalk dust.

   _____

Drawing Conclusions

1. What happened to the sandpaper and the chalk?

The piece of chalk became smaller. The sandpaper had chalk dust on it.

2. Which material changed more? Tell why you think this happened.

The chalk changed more because it was softer than the sandpaper. The sand

in the sandpaper rubbed against and broke off small pieces of the chalk.

3. Infer What might happen when strong winds blow over rocks? How would the rocks change?

Over time, the wind and sand could wear down the rocks.

4. FURTHER INQUIRY Experiment What changes might you see in the chalk if it is left outside for a week or more? Why? Do an experiment to test your ideas.

Students will probably observe the chalk crumble because it will be exposed

to the elements.

Inquiry

Think of your own questions that you might like to test. How else might rocks be worn down?

My Question Is:

Possible question: Are rocks worn down by water that freezes and thaws?

How I Can Test It:

Possible answer: I can observe what happens when I freeze and thaw wet chalk

several times.

My Results Are:

Possible answer: Cracks form in chalk when water in it freezes and thaws.

Alternative Explore
Lesson 7

Other Changes

Procedure

Materials
• pieces of chalk

1. Work with your group to make a list of ways that you think natural events could change the shape of a piece of chalk.

2. List your group's ideas.

   Possible answer: Heavy rains, strong winds, or moving water could wear

   down the chalk.

3. Select one of your group's ideas and research it.

4. If you want to test your idea, plan an experiment to test it. Write your plan on another sheet of paper. Have your teacher check your plan before you try your experiment.

Drawing Conclusions

1. What idea did you decide to research?

   Possible answer: Moving water could wear down the chalk.

2. How did you research it?

   Possible answer: We placed chalk under running water from a jar. (children

   should collect the water and use it over and over again)

3. What were your results?

   Possible answer: Running water wears down chalk.

Changing Chalk

Hypothesize Vinegar is a kind of chemical. What will happen when chalk is put in vinegar?

Write a **Hypothesis:**

Possible hypothesis: The vinegar will soften the chalk.

Materials

- apron
- safety goggles
- piece of chalk
- cup
- vinegar

Procedure

BE CAREFUL! Wear goggles and an apron.

1. Look at a piece of chalk. Describe it. Make a drawing of it on a piece of paper.

2. Place a piece of chalk in a cup. Add just enough vinegar to cover the chalk.

3. **Observe** Watch the chalk. Draw and describe what you see.

There were some bubbles and some of the

chalk disappeared..

Drawing Conclusions

4. Remove the chalk from the cup. How did the vinegar change the chalk? What properties of the chalk are different from before? Draw a picture of it.

The vinegar worked to dissolve the chalk.

5. Could chemicals like vinegar weather rocks? How do you know?

Yes. It can make them crumble into pieces like the chalk. The chalk is made

of a mineral called calcite.

Form a Hypothesis

Which Materials Settle First?

What happens to materials that are carried away by erosion? In this activity, you will model an experiment that finds the answer. The first step in the experiment is to form a hypothesis. A hypothesis is an answer to a question that can be tested.

My **Hypothesis:**

Possible answer: The solid materials will settle to the bottom

of the jar.

Materials

- large plastic jar with a lid
- measuring cup
- pebbles
- sand
- soil
- water

Procedure

1. **Observe** Look at the pebbles, soil, and sand. Describe each one of these materials. How do they compare with one another?

   They differ in size and color.

2. **Form a Hypothesis** When pebbles, sand, and soil are mixed together with water, how do they settle? Which material forms the bottom layer? Which forms the top? Form a hypothesis that answers these questions.

   The larger particles will fall to the bottom. The smaller ones will be on top.

3. **Experiment** Pour one cup of each material into the jar. Fill the jar almost to the top with water. Seal the jar tightly with a lid. Shake the jar.

4. **Observe** Let the jar sit for several hours. Observe the contents of the jar. Record your observations.

Students will notice that the water at the top of the jar becomes clearer as the suspended dirt settles out. They will also notice that the top layer of settled material becomes thicker.

Drawing Conclusions

1. Compare the results of the experiment with your hypothesis. Did the results support your hypothesis?

At first, the contents of the jar looked muddy and mixed up. Then the sand, soil, and pebbles formed layers. Students should judge if their hypotheses were correct.

2. Which material settled first? Which materials settled second and last? How do you know?

The pebbles settled first, the sand settled second, and the soil settled last. You know this because of where the layers are in the jar.

3. **Interpret Data** Repeat this activity. Compare these results with the results from the first time. What happened when you repeated the activity? Compare your findings with a classmate's. What did you find out? Summarize your findings.

Students' findings should be similar to the first experiment. The heavier materials settled first: the pebbles first, the sand second, and the soil last.

© Macmillan/McGraw-Hill

How Do Gentle and Heavy Rains Change Earth's Land?

Materials
- 2 trays
- soil and sand mixture
- water
- spray bottle
- cup

Procedure: Design Your Own

1. **Make a Model** Pour equal amounts of the mixture into two trays. At one end of each tray, pat the mixture to model a hill. Make both hills alike. Draw a picture of the two lands you modeled. Use separate paper.

2. **Form a Hypothesis** Do gentle or heavy rains change Earth's land more? Work with a classmate. Decide on a plan to test your hypothesis, using available materials.

   Heavy rains cause more changes than gentle rains. Use the spray bottle for
   light rain and model heavy rain by pouring water from a cup.

3. **Experiment** Carry out your plan. Draw the two lands as they look at the end of the experiment. Draw them on separate paper.

Drawing Conclusions

1. How do the two lands you modeled compare?

   The model that got heavy rain should be flatter than the model that got
   gentle rain.

2. Which kind of rainfall causes more erosion?

   heavy rain

3. **FURTHER INQUIRY** **Observe** You experimented on model landforms. How do you think your results compare with changes in the real world? Observe changes in the land after gentle and heavy rains. Compare these examples of erosion to changes in this activity. Write on a separate piece of paper.

   Answers will vary.

© Macmillan/McGraw-Hill

Alternative Explore

Lesson 8

More Rain

Procedure

1. In each tray, mix soil and rocks. Using the other materials, make a model of a city, a desert, or a forest. The land in both trays should look the same.

2. Use each pencil to poke holes in a different paper cup. One pencil should be thicker than the other.

3. Hold the cups over the trays and pour water into them, to make it "rain" on your land.

4. Observe how the two kinds of rain affect your land. Record your observations.

   Answers may vary depending on the landscapes. The

   heavier rainfall should cause the greatest change.

   _____

Materials

- 2 paper cups
- soil
- 2 large trays
- small and large rocks
- 2 pencils with different widths
- plants
- measuring cup
- water
- plastic containers

Drawing Conclusions

1. What happened when it rained?

   Some of the soil washed to the other side of the tray.

   _____

2. How do other objects affect the amount of erosion that occurs?

   Plants and buildings block the flow of water and soil, so they stop soil from

   washing downhill.

Weather Adds Up

Hypothesize Some cities have a lot of rain each year. Other cities only have a little. In which kind of a city will a stone monument change more quickly?

Possible hypothesis: It will change more quickly where there is a lot of rain.

Procedure

1. **Interpret Data** Look at the table on page C71 of your textbook. What is the difference in winter temperatures between the two cities? Which city has more rainfall?

   15 degrees; New York City

Drawing Conclusions

2. Add weather information about the place where you live. How does the weather in each city compare with the weather where you live?

   Answers will vary depending on students' location.

3. **Infer** A stone monument was moved to New York City from Egypt. The surface of the monument changed very quickly in New York. Why do you think this happened?

   In New York, the monument was subjected to more rain and lower winter temperatures than in Egypt. Rain enters cracks in the monument and soaked into the surface, froze, and cracked the monument.

4. **Going Further** Does the material a monument is made of affect how much it changes? Explain your answer.

   Yes, some materials are softer and may have more holes in the surface than others.

How Can You Show That Air Is Real?

Procedure

1. Fill the container about half full with water. Put a dry paper towel completely inside the cup.

2. Hold the cup upside down. Push the cup to the bottom of the container. Be careful not to tilt the cup.

3. **Observe** Remove the cup from the water. Remember to be careful not to tilt the cup. Look at the towel. Record your findings.

   The towel stayed dry.

4. **Observe** Again, hold the cup upside down, and push it to the bottom of the container. This time slowly tilt the cup. Record your findings.

   The towel got wet.

Materials

- plastic container
- plastic cup
- water
- paper towels

Drawing Conclusions

1. What happened to the towel in step 3? In step 5?

   The towel stayed dry in step 3. In step 5, the towel got wet.

   _____

2. What keeps water from filling the cup? _____ air _____

3. Is air real? How can you tell? _____ Yes, because air takes up space. _____

4. FURTHER INQUIRY **Communicate** How would this activity work on the moon? Explain.

   Possible answers: When pushed down into water, the cup would completely

   fill with water. The moon has no air, so air would not be trapped in the

   upside down cup.

©Macmillan/McGraw-Hill

Watching Air Move

Procedure

Materials

- talcum powder
- fan (optional)

1. Stir up the air in your classroom by running a fan or blowing and waving your arms. Can you see the air moving? Why or why not?

   No, air is invisible.

2. Put a little bit of talcum powder on your palm. Gently blow on the powder. How does the powder move?

   The powder scatters high in the air. Then it slowly drifts down

   toward the ground.

Drawing Conclusions

1. How does air move? How did the powder help you see how air moves?

   Air moves from one place to another. You can see how this happens

   by watching the powder move through the air.

2. Suppose you do step 2 again, but this time you blow on the powder as hard as you can. What do you think will happen?

   Possible answer: The powder will move through the air faster

   than it did before.

Mighty Air

Hypothesize How can you show that air pressure exists?

Write a **Hypothesis:**

Possible hypothesis: The air pressure increases when an

object has more surface exposed to the air.

Procedure

1. Place a ruler on a desk. Half of the ruler should be hanging off the edge of the desk. Draw the set up on a piece of paper.

2. **Observe** Carefully hit the edge of the ruler that is hanging off the desk with your hand. What happens?

    The ruler will move, and possibly fall off the table.

3. Cover the ruler with a page of newspaper.

Drawing Conclusions

4. **Predict** What do you think will happen when the ruler is hit? Record your predictions.

    Answers will vary.

5. **Observe** Hit the ruler again. What happens? Write down your findings.

    Students should find that the weight of air pressing on the newspaper

    keeps the ruler in place when they hit it again.

© Macmillan/McGraw-Hill

How Do Raindrops Form?

Hypothesize How can you make a model of Earth to show how raindrops form?

Write a **Hypothesis:**

Possible hypothesis: Set up a terrarium with a lid and look for

water in the terrarium to condense on the inside of the lid.

Procedure

1. Fill the jar one-fourth of warm water.

2. Place plastic wrap over the top of the jar.
   Use a rubber band to seal the wrap to the jar.

3. Set a marble in the center of the plastic wrap.

4. **Make a Model** Place several small pieces of ice on top of the plastic wrap. You have made a model of Earth. The warm water represents a lake, and the air above it represents the air around Earth.

5. **Observe** Carefully watch the bottom of the plastic wrap. Record your observations.

   Drops of water form on the bottom of the plastic wrap.

   _____

Materials

- clear-plastic jar
- plastic wrap
- rubber band
- marble
- ice cubes
- warm water

Drawing Conclusions

1. What did you see inside the jar?

Drops of water form on the bottom of the plastic wrap.

2. Where did the water come from to make the raindrops?

The warm water in the jar evaporated and then cooled

to form drops under the plastic wrap.

3. Infer Do you think water might go into the air faster during the
day or the night? Why?

The water would go into the air faster during the day, when it is

warmer, than the night.

4. FURTHER INQUIRY Infer What do you think would have happened if
you had poured cold water into the jar instead of warm water? Try it.

Drops are less likely to have formed, since the greater the difference

between the two temperatures, the greater the chance of condensation.

Inquiry

Think of your own questions that you might like to test. What happens to
the raindrops after they fall to Earth? Write and conduct an experiment.

My Question Is:

Possible question: Where do raindrops go after they fall?

_____

How I Can Test It:

Possible test: Take the plastic wrap off the cup. Observe what happens to

the water.

My Results Are:

After several hours the water begins to disappear.

_____

© Macmillan/McGraw-Hill

Drops on the Can

Procedure

Materials

- clean, dry empty food can
- water
- ice cubes
- red marker

1. Fill the can with a lot of ice and a little water.

2. Watch the outside of the can. What happens after about 30 minutes?

   Beads of water form on the can.

   _____

3. Now use the marker to mark the water line on the outside of the can.

4. Wait 24 hours. Where is the water compared to the water line on the can?

   The water is below the water line.

   _____

Drawing Conclusions

1. Where did the water that formed the water drops on the can come from?

   The water drops came from the air.

   _____

2. How might the can look on a more humid day?

   More water drops will form on the can.

   _____

3. What happened to the water in the can after 24 hours?

   The water evaporated into the air.

   _____

Make a Model and Infer

How Does Temperature Affect Evaporation?

Does the temperature of the air affect evaporation? How could you find out? In this activity you will make a model and then infer to investigate this question.

Materials
- water
- 2 plastic cups
- marker

Procedure

1. **Make a Model** Fill each cup half full with water. Use the marker to show where the water level is.

2. Place one cup in a warm place. Place the other cup in a cool place.

3. **Predict** In which cup will the water level change the most? Record your prediction.

   Students may predict either cup.
   _____

4. **Observe** Look at the cups every day for one week. Measure the water depth in the cups. Record your measurements. How did the amount of water change?

   More water evaporated from the cup in the warm place than the
   one in the cool place.
   _____

© Macmillan/McGraw-Hill

● Drawing Conclusions

1. Infer Where did the water in each cup go?

The water evaporated into the air.

2. How did the amount of water differ after two days?

The cup in the warm place had less water in it than the cup in the cool place.

3. How does this compare with your prediction?

Students should state that it was the same as or different from

their prediction.

4. Infer How could you use this model to make seawater drinkable?

One way to make seawater drinkable would be to evaporate

the water, collect the gas, and condense it again. The salt would be left

behind and the condensation would be fresh water.

How Do You Measure Temperature?

Materials

• thermometer

Procedure

1. **Predict** Where do you think the air temperature in your classroom is the highest and the lowest? Record your predictions.

   Accept any reasonable answer.

2. **Measure** Use a thermometer to find the air temperature at several places in the classroom. Then read and record the temperature. Remember to include the places in your predictions.

   Check that students are recording measurements clearly and accurately.

3. How did your measurements compare with your predictions?

   Answers will vary.

Drawing Conclusions

1. What was the warmest spot in your classroom? What was the coolest spot in your classroom?

   Check that students choose the warmest and coolest spots.

2. **Communicate** Use the measurements to make a bar graph on a separate piece of paper. Check that graphs accurately reflect the data.

3. **FURTHER INQUIRY** **Predict** What if you were doing this activity outside? Predict where you think the air temperature would be the highest and the lowest. Test your predictions.

   Possible answers include sunny, calm areas might be the warmest; shaded, windy areas might be the coolest.

© Macmillan/McGraw-Hill

Temperatures in the Classroom

Procedure

1. Find the five spots in your classroom where a thermometer is taped.

2. Without looking at the thermometers, predict what temperature each shows. Record your predictions in the chart below.

3. Now read the temperature on each of the five thermometers. Record the temperatures in the chart.

Materials

• thermometers

Thermometer	Predictions	Recorded Temperatures
One		
Two		
Three		
Four		
Five		

Drawing Conclusions

1. Which spot had the highest temperature? Why?

   The sunny spot had the highest temperature. It receives much heat from the sun.

2. Which spot had the lowest temperature? Why?

   The shady spot had the lowest temperature. It receives less heat from the sun than the sunny spot.

3. How might the spots with the highest and lowest temperatures compare at nighttime? Why?

   The temperatures would be the same in both spots. At night, the sunny and shady spots are both in darkness.

Rain Gauge

Hypothesize How can you measure rainfall?

Write a **Hypothesis:**

Possible hypothesis: Use a container to catch the rain and

measure the amount.

Materials

- plastic jar
- 6-inch paper ruler
- tape

Procedure

1. Use a plastic jar as a rain gauge. Tape a six-inch paper ruler to the jar. Make sure the ruler is straight up and down. Zero should be at the bottom of the jar.

2. When it is going to rain, place your jar in an open area where it can collect rain. Don't put the jar near or under trees or near buildings.

Drawing Conclusions

3. **Observe** After it rains, see how much rain fell. Try to measure to the nearest eighth of an inch.

   Make sure students are reading their measurements correctly.

4. **Measure** Record the amount of rainfall. Do this for several rains.

   Amounts will vary.

© Macmillan/McGraw-Hill

What Causes Day and Night?

Hypothesize How can you make a model to show what causes day and night?

Write a **Hypothesis**:

Possible hypothesis: Using a light source and a ball or globe,

one could model the Sun's light and Earth.

Materials

- globe

- medium self-stick notes

- flashlight

Procedure

1. Write *I live here* on a self-stick note. Place the note over the United States on the globe. While one person holds the globe, shine the flashlight on the self-stick note.

2. **Observe** If the flashlight is the Sun, would it be day or night on the self-stick note? Is it day or night on the other side of the globe?

   When the flashlight shines on the note, it is day where the note

   is and night on the other side of the globe.

3. Think of two different ways to make it night at the place near the self-stick note.

   Students can turn the globe, move the flashlight, or turn off the light.

   If students turn off the light, ask them if the Sun could really be turned off.

4. **Make a Model** Use the globe and the flashlight to test your ideas.

© Macmillan/McGraw-Hill

Drawing Conclusions

1. How did you create day and night in the first model and in the second model?

   Answers may vary, but most students will say that they turned the globe in

   the first model and moved or turned off the flashlight in the second.

2. Which idea do you think better explains what you know about day and night? Why?

   Students should justify their answers. Have them consider which model is

   the most realistic, based on prior knowledge about Earth and the Sun.

3. **FURTHER INQUIRY** **Infer** You put your wet sneakers in the sunlight to dry. An hour later they are in shade. How do you know what happened? Use your model to explain.

   As Earth rotated, the place where the sneakers were located turned

   away from the Sun.

Inquiry

Think of your own questions that you might like to test. What would happen if Earth rotated faster or slower? Write and conduct an experiment.

My Question Is:

Possible question: What would happen if Earth rotated faster or slower?

How I Can Test It:

Possible test: Spin a globe around for one minute. Spin the globe faster.

Spin it slower.

My Results Are:

Faster would mean shorter days. Slower would mean longer days.

Day or Night?

Procedure

Materials

- large globe
- modeling clay
- pencil
- lamp or flashlight

1. Work with a partner. Use the clay to make a small model of a person. Carefully attach the model to the pencil point.

2. One partner holds the free end of the pencil to a certain place on the globe.

3. The other partner shines a light at the globe. This light is like the light from the Sun. Is the model in day or night? How do you know?

   A model in the light is in day. A model in the dark is in night.

4. The partner holding the model should begin slowly rotating the globe. The model should always stay in the same location. Every once in a while, the movement should stop. For each stop, tell whether the model is in day or night.

   See answer for step 3.

5. When the globe completes one rotation, is the model in day or night?

   It should be the same as in the beginning of the rotation.

Drawing Conclusions

1. What causes day and night?

   Earth rotates around the Sun, creating day and night.

2. If you move the model to the opposite side of the globe, would the model now be in day or night?

   If the model was in day before, it would now be in night. If the model was

   in night before, it would now be in day.

Sundial

Hypothesize How can you measure the Sun's changing path in the sky? Write a **Hypothesis:**

Possible hypothesis: You can measure the Sun's changing

path in the sky by observing a shadow at different times of

the day and year.

Materials

- pencil
- marker
- paper taped to cardboard
- clay

Procedure

1. Tape a piece of paper to some cardboard. Use clay to anchor a pencil straight up at the center of the paper. Take your sundial outside at 9 A.M. on a sunny morning.

2. **Measure** Use a marker to draw a line through the middle of the pencil's shadow. Label the line with the time of day. Measure and mark the pencil's shadow again at 12 noon and 3 P.M.

3. Draw the Sun's position on a piece of paper.

Drawing Conclusions

4. How does the shadow's position change in one day? Is the Sun high or low in the sky when the shadows are the longest?

The shadow moves from one side of the paper to the other. The

shadows are longest when the Sun is low in the sky.

©Macmillan/McGraw-Hill

How Does the Moon's Shape Change?

Hypothesize You know that the Moon does not always look the same. Can a sphere look like a different shape without actually changing its shape?

Write a **Hypothesis:**

Possible hypothesis: The different shape has something to do with

the movement of Earth or the Moon.

Materials

- lamp
- volleyball

Procedure

1. **Observe** From your seat, look at the ball closely. Draw the ball.

2. **Make a Model** Turn off the classroom lights. Turn on the lamp and shine it on one side of the ball. Draw the shape of the ball where the light hits it.

3. **Infer** Compare all the drawings. What do you think caused the different shapes?

   Drawings should show a variety of shapes from thin slice to half circle to

   whole circle. Students sitting next to each other should have more similar

   drawings than those sitting far apart.

Drawing Conclusions

1. How did the ball look when you first observed it? How did it look in the darkened room?

   Answer: It looked like a round ball at first. Answers will vary according to

   where the student sat in the darkened room. Possible answer: It looked

   like a thin slice.

2. Why did your classmates see different lighted shapes?

  Because only part of the sphere was lit, its shape

  appeared to be different depending on where one sat.

3. **Infer** In this model the ball is the Moon and the lamp is the Sun. What are you? _____Earth_____

4. FURTHER INQUIRY **Infer** Why does the Moon appear to change its shape? How do you know?

  People on Earth view the Moon from different positions. That means they

  see different portions of it lit up.

Inquiry

Think of your own questions that you might like to test using the lamp and volleyball. What would happen if you changed the position of the lamp or ball?

My Question Is:

Possible answer: How will my view of the ball change if the lamp

changes position?

How I Can Test It:

Possible answer: I can change the position of the lamp and then draw

my view of the ball.

My Results Are:

Possible answer: Answers will vary, but the view of the ball will

have changed.

© Macmillan/McGraw-Hill

Seeing Hemispheres

Procedure

1. Use a different marker to color half of each rubber ball.

2. Place the balls on your desk so they do not roll.

3. Observe the shape of the colored parts of the balls that face you. Draw the shape of the colored part of one of the balls in the space below.

4. Turn the same ball you drew slightly. Observe the shape of the colored part that faces you now. Draw its shape in the space below.

5. Repeat step 4 two times. Student drawings will depend on the positions of the ball, but should show shapes similar to those of the phases of the Moon.

Materials
- small rubber balls
- different colored markers

Drawing Conclusions

How did the half of the ball you colored appear to change shape?

Its shape appeared to change because different amounts of the _____

colored half of the ball were visible with each turn. _____

Predict

Use Patterns

Rachel observed the Moon on different days during one month. She drew her observations on this calendar. There were some days she did not observe the Moon. Can you predict the shape of the Moon on the days she did not observe it?

Procedure

1. **Observe** Study the calendar below.

2. Look for similar shapes and patterns of the Moon.

JANUARY						
Sunday	Monday	Tuesday	Wednesday	Thursday	Friday	Saturday
		1	2	3	4	5
6	7	8	9	10	11	12
13	14	15	16	17	18	19
20	21	22	23	24	25	26
27	28	29	30	31		

Drawing Conclusions

1. **Predict** What do you think the Moon's shape was on Wednesday, January 9? Compare it with the shape of the Moon on January 8 and January 11. Draw your prediction.

Drawings should show a crescent with points toward the left that is fatter than the January 8 crescent but slimmer than the January 11 one.

2. **Predict** What was the Moon's shape on Friday, January 25? Compare it with the shape of the Moon on January 24 and January 26. Draw your prediction.

Drawings should show a fat crescent with points toward the right that is slimmer than January 24 but fatter than January 26.

3. **Predict** Draw the shape of the Moon you would expect to see on January 29. What helped you decide on that shape?

Drawings should show a very thin crescent with points toward the right.

Looking at the pictures for the days prior to January 29 helps you
decide on the shape.

4. **Observe** Observe the change in the shape of the moon in the sky for one month. Draw the shape in a calendar like the one shown on page 116. Describe how the pattern changes.

Students should show and describe the different phases of the moon.

How Do Planets Move?

Hypothesize You know that the Moon appears to change shape as it moves around Earth. You can observe other changes in the night sky, too—like the position of the planets. Why don't you see the planets in the same place every night?

Materials

- sign for each planet
- 2 signs for the Sun

Write a **Hypothesis:**

Possible hypothesis: The planets and Earth are both moving.

_____

_____

Procedure

1. **Make a Model** Take turns with other groups of classmates. Model the motion of the planets around the Sun. When you are not doing the modeling, make as many observations as you can.

2. **Observe** Listen to the student who is modeling Earth. He or she will describe what can be seen from Earth in the night sky.

Drawing Conclusions

1. What planets were visible from Earth the first time you modeled the motions of the planets? What planets were visible the second time?

   Answers will vary. Visible planets will depend on the positions of

   the students.

© Macmillan/McGraw-Hill

2. How did Earth's motion affect what planets could be seen from Earth? How did the motion of the other planets affect what planets could be seen from Earth?

Possible answer: The Earth and the planets are always moving.

Because of this nonstop movement, what we can see changes.

3. Why does the position of the planets in the night sky change?

Possible answer: The position of the planets in the night sky

changes as Earth and the other planets revolve around the Sun.

4. FURTHER INQUIRY Observe How would the position of Venus change in your model if you moved faster or slower around the Sun? Use your model to test your ideas.

A change in the speed of any of the planets could change which

planets we can see from Earth.

Inquiry

Think of your own questions that you might like to test using the signs for the Sun and the planets. If you lived on another planet, which planets can be seen from your home in the night sky?

My Question Is:

Possible answer: Which planets in the night sky can be seen from Mars?

How I Can Test It:

Possible answer: One group will model the motion of the planets around the

Sun. The student who is modeling Mars will share with the class what can be

seen in the night sky.

My Results Are:

Answers will vary.

Planet Movement

Procedure

Materials

- clay
- paper
- marker

1. Make a model of the solar system. First, make a Sun out of clay. Place it in the center of the paper.

2. Draw 9 circles around the Sun, representing the paths of the planets.

3. Use clay to make the planets, and place each one on its path around the Sun.

4. Imagine you are on Earth looking up at the night sky. List those planets you could see if they were in the positions you just placed them in.

Answers will depend on planet positions.
_____

_____

5. Move each planet a different distance along its path around the Sun. List those planets you could now see if you were on Earth looking up at the night sky.

Answers will depend on planet positions.
_____

_____

Drawing Conclusions

Could you see the same planets each time? Why or why not?

Answers should indicate that the planets you can see depends on

where the planets are along their orbits relative to Earth's night side.
_____

_____

©Macmillan/McGraw-Hill

Make a Letter Larger

Hypothesize How does the shape of lenses change how objects look?

Write a **Hypothesis:**

Possible hypothesis: Curved lenses magnify faraway objects.

Materials

- dropper
- newspaper
- water
- masking tape
- paper cup
- wax paper

Procedure

1. Cover a piece of newspaper with some wax paper.

2. **Observe** Put a small drop of water over a letter. How does it look?

   It looks bigger.

3. **Experiment** Put water drops of different sizes over other letters. Observe.

Drawing Conclusions

4. How does the size of the drop affect the way the print looks?

   Small drops are more curved and magnify the print more than big drops.

5. **Infer** How is the curved lens in a telescope like the drop of water?

   A curved lens acts like a curved water drop. The lens magnifies
   the faraway object.

How Fast Do You Move?

Hypothesize How much faster do you run than walk?
How might you test your ideas? Write a **Hypothesis:**

Possible hypothesis: I run twice as fast as I walk.

Materials

• stopwatch
• red crayon
• blue crayon
• graph paper
• meter tape

Procedure

1. **Measure** Measure and mark 10 meters on the
   floor using the meter tape.

2. **Predict** Predict and record how long you think it
   will take each group member to walk 10 meters and to
   run 10 meters.

   Predictions will vary.

3. **Measure** Have each person walk 10 meters. Use the stopwatch to
   measure each person's time. Record each time.

   Answers will vary.

4. Have each person run 10 meters. Measure and record each
   person's time.

   Answers will vary.

● Drawing Conclusions

1. Make a bar graph like the one shown in your textbook on page E5. Use the blue crayon to show walking time. Use the red crayon to show running time. Make a key, and name your graph.

   Graphs should reflect that running time was shorter than walking time.

2. Repeat the activity. What is the difference, in seconds, between the first time you ran and the second?

   Answers will depend on each child's results.

3. FURTHER INQUIRY Predict How would the times change if you walked uphill and then downhill? How do you know?

   Possible answer: It would take longer walking uphill. It is harder to walk

   uphill than downhill.

Inquiry

Think of your own questions that you might like to test. For example: How would the slope of a hill affect how far you travel?

My Question Is:

Possible question: Does walking uphill make me walk slower?

How I Can Test It:

Possible test: I can time how long it takes me to walk 10 meters uphill and

compare this time to my earlier results.

My Results Are:

Possible answer: Moving uphill slows me down.

How Far, How Fast

Procedure

Materials

- stopwatch
- red crayon
- blue crayon
- graph paper
- meter tape

1. **Measure** Use a stopwatch and time how far each member of your group can walk in 5 seconds. Record each distance.

   Students should walk in a straight line. Have students
   round off the distance to the meter.

2. **Measure** Time how far each member of your group can run in 5 seconds. Record each distance.

   Students should run in a straight line. Caution students not to run too fast.

Drawing Conclusions

1. Make a bar graph using your results. Draw a line on the bottom of a piece of graph paper. Write "walking" and "running" next to each other below the drawn line. On one column above "walking" color one box in red for every meter you walked. On another column above "running" color one box in blue for every meter you ran.

2. **Compare** Did you walk or run further in 5 seconds? What is the difference in meters?

   Students most likely ran further in 5 seconds than they walked.
   Difference in meters will vary.

3. **Predict** Use your bar graph to predict how far you would walk in 20 seconds.

   Students should quadruple their distance in 20 seconds. Twenty
   seconds is four times as long as 5 seconds.

QUICK LAB
FOR SCHOOL OR HOME
Lesson 1

Measuring Distance

Hypothesize What will happen to a piece of crumpled paper when you blow on it? Will it move? Or will it stay in the same position? Write a **Hypothesis:**

Possible hypothesis: The paper will move forward

when I blow on it.

_____

Materials

- 2 rulers
- paper
- block
- pencil
- marble

Procedure

1. Place one ruler on the floor to mark a starting line.

2. **Experiment** Set a crumpled piece of paper in front of the ruler. Take a breath and blow the paper as far as you can.

3. **Measure** Use another ruler to find the distance the paper moved. Record the number.

   Answers will vary.

4. Repeat steps 2 and 3 using a block, a pencil, and a marble.

   Answers will vary.

5. Which object traveled the greatest distance?

   Lighter objects travel farther than heavier ones.

Drawing Conclusions

6. Which of the objects changed position?

The paper, pencil, and marble will most likely have changed positions.

_____

_____

7. Which of the objects did not change position?

The block did not move.

_____

8. Why do you think some objects moved farther than others?

Possible answer: Some objects may have been blown harder than

others. Some objects are lighter than others.

_____

9. Going Further Pick three additional objects in the room. Predict which object will move the farthest. Predict which object will move the least. Write your predictions, then test your objects.

Answers will vary depending on the objects chosen.

_____

_____

_____

_____

Why Are Some Objects Harder to Pull?

Hypothesize Why are some objects harder to push or pull than others? How might you test your ideas? Write a **Hypothesis:**

Possible hypothesis: Some objects are heavier than others, which makes them harder to push or pull.

Materials

- spring scale
- safety goggles
- 5 objects of about the same size

Procedure **BE CAREFUL!** Wear goggles.

1. **Observe** What is the highest the spring scale can read?

   Answers will vary depending on the scale.

2. **Predict** Which object will need the strongest pull to move it? Record your prediction.

   Predictions will vary. The heaviest objects will require the greatest pull.

3. **Predict** Which object will need the next strongest pull to move it? Record your prediction. Do the same for the rest of the objects.

   Answers will vary.

4. Hook the scale on an object. Pull the scale and the object along a smooth, flat surface.

5. **Measure** Measure and record what the spring scale reads. Do the same for all the objects.

   Answers will vary.

6. Compare your predictions with your measurements.

   Answers will vary. The accuracy of predictions will vary.

Drawing Conclusions

1. What did you feel when you pulled on an object with the spring scale?

Children should feel a pull in the opposite direction.

2. Which objects made the scale read highest?

The heavier objects made the scale read the highest.

3. Why did you need a stronger pull to move some objects?

Bigger, heavier objects need a bigger push or pull to move them.

4. **FURTHER INQUIRY** **Experiment** How could you measure the size of the pull needed to move a lunchbox?

By using the spring scale in the same way as for the five objects

already measured.

Inquiry

Think of your own questions that you might like to test. Does the size of an object affect the amount of pull needed to move it?

My Question Is:

Possible question: Which of two objects requires more strength to lift?

How Can I Test It?

Possible test: I can repeat the activity, this time lifting two objects of

different sizes.

My Results Are:

Possible results: The heavier object required more strength to lift.

Comparing Lifting Strength

Procedure BE CAREFUL! Wear goggles.

1. Attach one of the three objects to the hook.

2. Run the string over the rod.

3. Pull the string to raise the object. Observe how much strength you needed to raise the object. Record your observations.

   Students should describe the relative strength needed

   to raise the object

4. Remove the object from the hook. Repeat steps 1–3 with the other two objects.

   Students should describe the relative strength needed to raise each object.

5. On your desk, place the objects in order of the amount of strength you needed to raise them.

Drawing Conclusions

What object took the most strength to raise? Which took the least strength to raise?

Answers will vary depending on objects used. The heaviest object took the

most strength to raise and the lightest took the least strength to raise.

Materials

- rod suspended over a table
- hook on one end of a long, sturdy string
- three objects of different weights
- safety goggles

©Macmillan/McGraw-Hill

Interpret Data

Read a Bar Graph

The graph below is a bar graph. Each bar gives you information, or *data*. This bar graph shows a dog's weight on different planets. Along the left side are the planet names. At the bottom are weights in pounds. Look at the end of the bar labeled *Earth*. It lines up with 40 pounds. The dog weighs 40 pounds on Earth. Look at the bar labeled *Jupiter*. What number does it line up with? You are interpreting data when you answer this question.

Interpret the data in this graph. Use the data to answer the questions below.

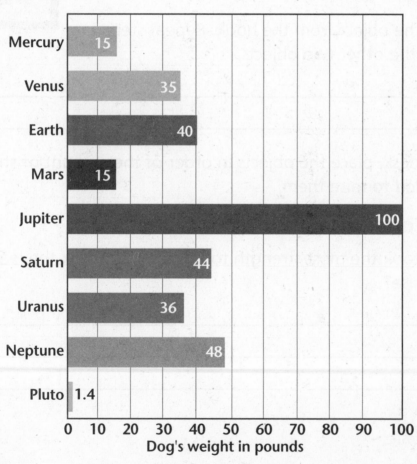

Dog's weight in pounds

© Macmillan/McGraw-Hill

Procedure

1. **Interpret Data** How much does the dog weigh on Mars?

   about 15 pounds

2. Interpret Data Where is the dog heavier than it is on Earth? Where is it lighter?

Jupiter, Saturn, and Neptune; Mercury, Venus, Mars, Uranus, and Pluto

3. Compare the dog's weight on Jupiter with its weight on Venus. How much heavier is it on Jupiter?

about 65 pounds heavier

Drawing Conclusions

Communicate How would your weight change if you visited the other planets?

It would become heavier on Jupiter, Saturn, and Neptune. It would become

lighter on Mercury, Venus, Mars, Uranus, and Pluto.

What Causes a Change in Motion?

Hypothesize Sometimes objects change position, and sometimes they stay still. What must you do to make a resting object move? How might you test your ideas? Write a **Hypothesis:**

Possible hypothesis: You must push or pull a resting object to

make it move.

Materials

• washers

• 2 paper clips

• scissors

• string

• safety goggles

Procedure **BE CAREFUL!** Wear goggles.

1. Cut two pieces of string that are slightly shorter than the width of your desk. Knot the strings together.

2. Lay the knot in the middle of your desk. Let the strings hang off the opposite sides of the desk.

3. Bend the two paper clips into hooks. Tie a hook at the end of each hanging string.

4. Hold down the string at the knot.

5. **Predict** Hang two washers on one hook. Predict what will happen if you let go of the knot.

Predictions will vary.

6. **Experiment** Test your prediction. Record the results.

The knot moved.

7. **Experiment** Repeat steps 4, 5, and 6, this time hanging one washer on each hook.

Predictions will vary. The knot will stay in place.

©Macmillan/McGraw-Hill

Drawing Conclusions

1. **Communicate** Explain why the knot moved or did not move each time.

   The knot moves when the weight is heavier on one side. It stays in

   place when the weight is equal.

2. FURTHER INQUIRY **Form a Hypothesis** How could you move the knot in another direction?

   Students might suggest hanging more washers on one side.

   _____

   _____

Inquiry

Think of your own questions that you might like to test. Does changing the length of the string make a difference?

My Question Is:

Possible question: Does changing the length of the string make a difference?

_____

How I Can Test It:

Possible test: I can try changing the length of both sides of the string and one

side of the string and observe what happens.

My Results Are:

Possible answer: Changing both sides doesn't make a difference, but making

one side much longer does pull the knot toward that side.

Moving Hanger

Procedure BE CAREFUL! Wear goggles.

1. Push the bottom wire of the clothes hanger up so that the ends form two loops.

2. Hang the wire hanger from a rod.

3. Bend the paper clips open so they form hooks. Attach a paper clip hook to each loop of the wire hanger.

4. Hang two washers on one of the paper clip hooks. Observe what happens and record your observations.

   The hanger moves, tilting to one side.

5. Hang two washers on the other paper clip hook. Observe what happens and record your observations.

   The hanger tilts to the other side and balances.

Materials

- wire clothes hanger
- rod
- 2 paper clips
- washers
- safety goggles

Drawing Conclusions

1. How could you make one end of the hanger tilt?

   Put more washers on one side than the other.

2. How could you balance the sides of the hanger?

   Remove the washers or hang the same number of washers from each side.

©Macmillan/McGraw-Hill

QUICK LAB
FOR SCHOOL OR HOME
Lesson 3

Marbles in Motion

Hypothesize How can marbles help you reduce friction? Write a **Hypothesis:**

Possible hypothesis: Marbles are slippery objects that don't

rub well and produce little friction.

Procedure

Materials

- 10–20 marbles
- jar lid
- wooden block

1. **Observe** Push a wooden block across your desk. Describe how it feels.

   There is friction between the wooden block and the desk.

2. **Experiment** Place five marbles under the jar lid. Lay the block on top of the lid.

3. **Observe** Push the block across your desk again. Describe how it feels.

   There is less friction and the block moves across the desk easily.

4. Describe how the marbles helped reduce friction.

   Marbles are slippery and only a small area of their surfaces touched the lid.

Drawing Conclusions

5. **Communicate** When did you feel more friction:
When you pushed the block by itself or over the jar lid?

There was more friction when I pushed the block by itself.

6. **Going Further** What would happen if you placed a piece of sand-paper under the block and tried to push it across your desk?

The sandpaper is rough and it would increase friction.

© Macmillan/McGraw-Hill

What Is Work?

Hypothesize What do you think work is? In your own words, write a definition of work. How might you apply your definition of work to different kinds of actions? Write a **Hypothesis:**

Possible hypothesis: Work is getting things done; doing

chores at home; going to the office.

Materials

• 4 books

• pencil

Procedure

1. Complete each action described below.
   • Pick up one book.
   • Pick up four books at one time.
   • Put a book on your desk. Push down very hard on top of the book.
   • Push against a wall with all of your strength.

2. **Classify** After each action, ask yourself, "Did I do work?" Decide whether the action was work. Record your decision in the data chart shown.

   Students' decisions should be based on their definition of work.

Action	Work	Conclusion
Pick up one book	Work: Not work:	Why:

© Macmillan/McGraw-Hill

Drawing Conclusions

1. Evaluate your answers to the question "Did I do work?" Think about your answers. Is there a pattern? If so, what is it?

   One pattern students might identify is using their muscles in an activity.

2. Explain why you classified each action the way you did.

   The students might classify activities as work if they are difficult or require

   significant force, including pushing against a desk.

3. **FURTHER INQUIRY** **Define Terms** Picking up one, four, or any number of books from your desk is work. Use this information and your chart to tell what work is.

   Possible answer: Students may define work as an action, such as

   using energy to move something or moving parts of their bodies.

Inquiry

Think of your own questions that you might like to test. Is homework work?

My Question Is:

Possible question: Does homework involve work?

How I Can Test It:

Possible test: I can observe what I do while doing homework.

My Results Are:

Possible answer: Since homework involves some muscular force, it is work.

What Is Work?

Procedure

1. Form a group of four students.

2. Name an activity or action that you think is work.
   Record your activity or action.

   Students might categorize activities as work if they are difficult or

   require significant force, such as pushing against a desk.

3. For the members of your group, act out or describe your chosen
   activity or action. Explain why you think it is work.

4. Observe and record the examples and explanations of the other
   group members.

   Answers will vary.

   _____

Drawing Conclusions

1. What patterns did you find among your group's examples of work?
   How are they alike?

   Answers will depend on examples of work, but might include actions

   that require muscular force.

2. What do you now think work is?

   Accept all reasonable responses.

   _____

Changing Energy

Hypothesize What happens to the food you eat inside your body? Write a **Hypothesis:**

Possible hypothesis: It changes into energy.

_____

Materials
- food chart
- activity chart

Procedure

1. Your body needs energy. The table below shows the amount of energy in some of the foods we eat.

2. **Use Numbers** Using the table, plan a lunch. How many calories was your lunch? Record the information.

Answers will vary.

Food	Energy in Calories
2% chocolate milk	220
Low fat yogurt	230
Tuna Salad	190
Pizza	320

3. **Interpret Data** Pick some of the activities you enjoy. How long would you need to do them in order to use the energy from your lunch? Record the information.

Answers will vary but should be reasonable.

Activity	Calories Burned in 30 Minutes
Biking (slow)	35
Jogging	85
Fast walking	65
Listening to music	25

© Macmillan/McGraw-Hill

Drawing Conclusions

4. Use Numbers How much time jogging would it take to burn off a low fat yogurt?

about 90 minutes

5. Infer Why is it important to keep track of how much you eat and how much activity you do?

It can help you figure out a balanced diet and how to stay active to keep

healthy.

6. Going Further Plan a dinner with your favorite foods. Find the calories for the complete meal. Then figure out how long it would take for you to burn the calories using the activities on the chart.

Answers will vary.

©Macmillan/McGraw-Hill

How Can You Make Work Easier?

Hypothesize Sometimes you want to move an object that takes a lot of force to move. How can you do it? How might you test your ideas? Write a **Hypothesis:**

Students might suggest using a pulley.

_____

Materials

- roll of masking tape
- safety goggles
- building materials

Procedure: Design Your Own

BE CAREFUL! Wear goggles.

1. Invent a way to get the roll of tape from the floor to your desk. Your hands can help provide the lift, but you can't just pick up the tape.

2. **Communicate** Think of as many ways as you can to lift the tape. Share your ideas with your group members.

3. As a team, choose two plans and write them down. Remember to listen to each person's ideas.

   Students should clearly record their plans.

   _____

   _____

   _____

4. **Experiment** Place the roll of masking tape on the floor. Try to lift it. Write down what happens. Does the plan work well?

   Results will vary.

   _____

   _____

5. **Experiment** Try another plan.

© Macmillan/McGraw-Hill

Drawing Conclusions

1. Which plan worked better?

   Outcomes will vary, but the pairs should be able to explain why

   one plan worked better.

2. What materials did you use in your most successful invention?

   Students should list all the materials they used.

3. What forces did you use? What force did you work against?

   Forces used might include pushes, pulls, and/or friction. They

   were working against gravity.

4. **FURTHER INQUIRY** Experiment Would your plan work for lifting a small book? Explain your answer.

   Answers will vary.

Inquiry

Think of your own questions that you might like to test. If you had different materials, would you have been able to lift the tape?

My Question Is:

Possible question: Can I lift the tape using a pulley?

How I Can Test It:

Possible test: I can obtain a pulley and use it to try to lift the tape.

My Results Are:

Possible answer: I can lift the tape using a pulley.

Ways to Lift

Procedure BE CAREFUL! Wear goggles.

1. How could you move a washer from your desk into a paper cup without lifting it with your hands? Think of as many ways as you can to lift the washer.

2. Write or draw two of your plans in the space below. If you need more space, use a separate piece of paper.

Plans will vary, but should include the materials provided. Possible plans: Hook the washer on the string, tape the string to a tube, and wind the string on a tube. Make a pulley with string and a spool.

Materials

- washers
- paper cups
- scissors
- tape
- rulers
- paper clip hooks
- string
- paper tubes
- empty spools of thread
- safety goggles

3. After your teacher approves your plans, try one of them. Record what happens.

Answers should describe the success of the plan.
_____
_____

4. Try your other plan. Record what happens.

Answers should describe the success of the plan.
_____
_____

Drawing Conclusions

Which of your plans worked better? Why?

Students should describe the merits of one of their plans.
_____
_____

©Macmillan/McGraw-Hill

Make a Lever

Hypothesize What happens when you change the position of the fulcrum on a lever? Write a **Hypothesis:**

Possible hypothesis: If the fulcrum is farther from the load, more force is required to lift it.

_____

Materials

- clay
- ruler
- pencil
- 2 small blocks

Procedure

1. Use clay to hold a pencil in place on your desk. Place a ruler over the center of the pencil.

2. **Experiment** Put two blocks on one end of the ruler. Add pieces of clay to the other end of the ruler. How much clay does it take to lift the blocks?

   Answers will vary depending on the weight of the blocks and size of pieces of clay.

3. **Experiment** Change the position of the ruler on the pencil. Repeat step 2. How does the new position change your results?

   The closer the fulcrum is to the load, the less force is required to lift the load. The farther the fulcrum is from the load, the more force is required to lift the load.

Drawing Conclusions

4. Draw your lever in the space below. Label the force, load, and fulcrum.

The clay is the force, the blocks are the load, and the pencil is the fulcrum. The force pushing down on one end of the lever raises the load on the other end.

5. Going Further Name some levers that you have seen in action.

Possible answers: Wheelbarrow, seesaw, claw hammer, crowbar, nutcracker, broom, shovel

How Can a Ramp Make Work Easier?

Hypothesize When people built pyramids many years ago, they may have used a ramp to help them move rocks. How can a ramp make work easier? How might you test your ideas? Write a **Hypothesis:**

Children might suggest that ramps made the slopes more

gradual.

Materials

- 1-m wooden board
- spring scale
- thin spiral notebook
- 10-cm piece of string
- chair
- meter stick
- safety goggles

Procedure **BE CAREFUL!** Wear goggles.

1. Can you design a plan to find out if lifting an object straight up takes less force than pulling it up a ramp?

2. Tie one end of the string around the bottom of the spring scale. Tie the other end to the middle of the spiral wire of the notebook.

3. **Measure** Measure the pull needed to lift the notebook straight up to the height of the chair's seat. Then measure the distance you pulled the book. Record your measurements.

Students' measurements will vary.

_____

_____

4. **Measure** Lean one end of the wooden board on the chair. Measure the pull needed to move the notebook up the board to the seat of the chair. Then measure the distance you pulled the book. Record your measurements.

Measurements will vary.

_____

_____

© Macmillan/McGraw-Hill

Drawing Conclusions

1. Look at your measurements. Which method of moving the notebook required more force? Which method required moving the notebook a greater distance?

   Moving the notebook straight up required more force than moving

   it up at an angle. Moving at an angle required moving it a greater distance.

   _____

   _____

2. **FURTHER INQUIRY** **Infer** What happens if you change the angle of the board? How does this affect the amount of force needed to move the object?

   Possible answer: When the angle of the board is moved higher, the distance

   is shorter but steeper. When it is moved lower, the distance is longer and not

   as steep. It takes more force to move an object up the steeper angle.

© Macmillan/McGraw-Hill

Inquiry

Think of your own questions that you might like to test.
Does the roughness of a ramp's surface affect the force needed?

My Question Is:

Possible question: Does pulling an object on a rough surface take

more force than pulling on a smooth surface?

How I Can Test It:

Possible test: I can compare the forces needed to pull on both a

rough surface and a smooth surface.

My Results Are:

Possible answer: It takes more force to pull on a rough surface.

_____

Using a Ramp

Procedure

1. Stand next to the platform. Climb to the top of the platform by stepping straight up from the floor.

2. Use the meter stick to measure the distance you climbed. Record the distance.

   Answers will vary.

3. Stand at the base of the ramp. Climb to the top of the platform by walking up the ramp.

4. Use the meter stick to measure the distance you walked. Record the distance.

   Answers will vary.

Drawing Conclusions

1. Which route to the top of the platform covered a longer distance?

   the walk up the ramp

2. Which route would you rather take if you had to get on the platform many times a day? Explain your answer.

   Possible answer: I would rather walk up the ramp. Even though it was a longer distance, it took less work.

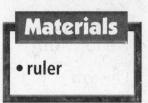
Use Numbers

Which Screw Makes Work Easiest?

You know that a screw is a simple machine. It makes work easier, just like any other inclined plane. It lets you use less force over a longer distance. Screws come in many shapes and sizes. Some screws make work easier than others.

The diagram here shows three screws. In this activity you will use numbers to evaluate how each screw is different. Then you will use that information to infer which screw makes work the easiest.

Materials

• ruler

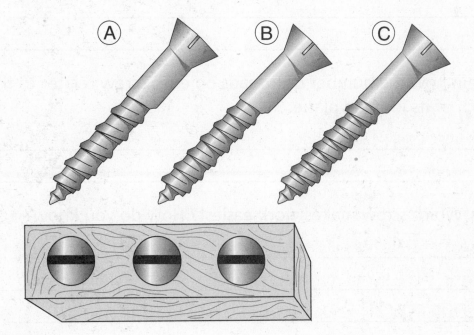

Procedure

1. **Measure** What is the width of each screw's head? What is the length of each screw?

2. Record your measurements in the table on the next page.

3. **Use Numbers** Count the number of threads on each screw.

4. Record the information in the table on the next page.

© Macmillan/McGraw-Hill

Screw	A	B	C
Head width	1.5 cm	1.5 cm	1.5 cm
Length	6 cm	6 cm	6 cm
Number of threads	6	7	8

Drawing Conclusions

1. How does the number of threads on each screw compare?

   The number of threads ranges from 6 to 8.

2. Explain how the number of threads on each screw relates to the length of its inclined plane.

   The more threads, the longer the inclined plane.

3. **Infer** Which screw makes work easiest? How do you know?

   The screw with 8 threads makes work easiest because it has the longest inclined plane. When you apply force over a longer distance less force is needed to do the work.

Which Object Takes Up More Space?

Hypothesize What will happen when you put different objects in a container of water? How might you test your ideas? Write a **Hypothesis:**

Possible hypothesis: The water level will rise when objects are added.

Materials

- plastic cup
- water
- markers
- piece of clay
- classroom objects

Procedure

1. **Predict** Look at the photograph. What will happen to the water level when you put the clay in the cup?

   Students will likely predict that the water level will rise.

2. **Measure** Half-fill the cup with water. Use a marker to mark the water level on the outside of the cup.

   Students should find the water level by viewing the cup at eye level.

3. **Observe** Place the clay in the cup. What happens? Mark the new water level. Use a different color.

   The water level goes up.

4. **Predict** Look at other objects. Which one will raise the water level most? Record your prediction.

   Students will likely predict that the largest object will cause the water to rise the most.

5. **Experiment** Add one object at a time to the cup. Mark the new water level each time. Use a different color.

Drawing Conclusions

1. **Infer** Which object takes up the most space? How do you know?

   The largest object takes up the most space. It caused the greatest change

   in the water level.

2. **FURTHER INQUIRY** **Experiment** What will happen to the water level in the cup if you change the shape of the clay?

   Nothing, because the clay will take up the same amount of space no matter

   what its shape.

Inquiry

Think of your own questions that you might like to test. Will a heavy object cause a greater change in the water level than lightweight objects? Write your question, a way to test your question, and your results on a separate sheet of paper.

My Question Is:

Possible question: Do two objects that are about the same size but different

weights cause the water level to rise the same amount?

How I Can Test It:

Possible test: Repeat the experiment using a coin and a plastic counter that are

about the same size.

My Results Are:

Possible results: The change in water level is the same. As long as the objects take

up the same amount of space, their weight does not affect the change in water

level.

© Macmillan/McGraw-Hill

Does Weight Matter?

Procedure

Materials

- 600-mL beaker
- water
- 3 regular golf balls and 3 plastic golf balls

1. Fill the beaker about half way with water. Measure and record the amount of water.

   Answers will vary.
   _____

2. Place the regular golf balls in the water. Record the level of the water. Remove the balls from the beaker.

   Answers will vary.
   _____

3. Place the plastic balls in the water. Hold them just under the surface. Record the level of the water. Remove the balls from the beaker.

   Answers will vary.
   _____

Drawing Conclusions

1. Which type of golf ball is heavier? Which takes up more space?

   The regular golf ball is heavier. Both types take up about the same amount
   of space.

2. Compare how high the water level rose with each type of ball. Explain your observations.

   Both types raised the water level about the same amount. Since they take
   up about the same amount of space but have different weights, the amount
   of space they take up must determine how high the water level rises.

Measuring Mass

Hypothesize Do objects in your classroom have different masses? Write a **Hypothesis:**

Possible hypothesis: Objects in the classroom have

different masses.

Materials

- balance
- 5 small objects
- 30 paper clips

Procedure

1. **Predict** Gather five small objects. Predict the mass of the objects. Record your predictions in the table below.

   Possible answer: Estimates depend on the objects selected and the student's reasoning.

2. **Measure** Measure the mass of each object. Place the object on one side of a balance. Add paper clips to the other side until the two sides balance. Record the number of paper clips used in the table.

3. **Use Numbers** What is the mass of each object in grams? (Two paper clips equal about one gram.)

Object	Number of Paper Clips	Mass of Object
	Mass in grams = (number of paper clips) divided by (2 paper clips per gram)	

© Macmillan/McGraw-Hill

Drawing Conclusions

4. Sort the objects from most mass to least mass.
   How do your results compare with your predictions? Explain on a separate piece of paper.

   The answers depend on student estimates and the objects tested.

5. What is the mass of all the objects combined? Explain your answer.

   Answers will vary according to the objects chosen.

6. **Going Further** A nickel equals about 5 grams. How can you use nickels to find the mass of objects in your classroom? Write and conduct an experiment.

   My Hypothesis Is:

   Possible hypothesis: You can use nickels to find the mass of objects by

   placing nickels on a balance until the two sides balance and then

   multiplying the number of nickels by 5.

   My Experiment Is:

   Possible experiment: Place an object on one side of the balance. Place

   nickels on the other side until the two sides balance. Record the number of

   nickels and multiply by 5.

   My Results Are:

   mass in grams = (number of nickels) multiplied by (5 grams per nickel)

How Can You Classify Matter?

Hypothesize How can you tell whether a material is a solid or a liquid? How might you test your ideas? Write a **Hypothesis:**

Possible hypothesis: You can tell if matter is a liquid or solid by observing its properties. Solids have a definite shape and volume, while liquids have a definite volume, but change shape freely.

Materials

- plastic container of Oobleck

- investigation tools

- newspaper

- safety goggles

Procedure: Design Your Own

BE CAREFUL! Wear goggles.

1. In your own words, define solids and liquids.

   Answers will vary.

2. **Observe** Use your senses to describe Oobleck. How does it look? What does it feel like? Record your observations.

   Possible answer: Oobleck looks green and it feels soft and wet.

3. **Experiment** Use the tools given to you to experiment with Oobleck. What new things do you observe? Record your observations.

   When a force is slowly applied to Oobleck it changes shape, but Oobleck resists changing shape when force is quickly applied.

4. **Classify** Review your definitions of solids and liquids. Would you classify Oobleck as a solid or a liquid? Explain your answer.

   Answers may vary. Accept all answers with logical reasoning, for example: Oobleck is a liquid because it can change shape.

© Macmillan/McGraw-Hill

Drawing Conclusions

1. **Communicate** What observations did you make about the properties of Oobleck?

   Students should describe the shape, smell, color, and texture of the

   substance. The shape is variable, the color is green, and the texture is soft

   and pasty. It should not have a strong smell.

2. How did you decide to classify Oobleck? What helped you make your decision?

   Explanations should refer to the properties of shape and volume. (Oobleck

   actually has the properties of both a solid and liquid.)

3. **FURTHER INQUIRY** **Form a Hypothesis** Does Oobleck have different properties at different temperatures? Design an experiment to find out.

   An Oobleck may be more stretchable and more like a liquid at higher

   temperatures. You could warm the Oobleck and observe its properties.

Inquiry

Think of your own questions that you might like to test. What else can you find out about Oobleck?

My Question Is:

Possible question: Is Oobleck a mixture of water and another substance?

How I Can Test It:

Possible test: Leave some Oobleck in an open container and see if it hardens.

My Results Are:

Possible answer: If Oobleck is left in an open container, the water will evaporate

and the substance will harden.

©Macmillan/McGraw-Hill

Changing Forms

Procedure

1. Observe the ice and water. Record their properties.

   <u>Possible properties: ice: cold, hard; water: warm, wet</u>

Materials

• ice cubes

• cups of water

2. Decide what type of matter the ice and water are, and explain your decision.

   <u>Students might indicate that the ice is a solid because it is hard and the</u>

   <u>water is a liquid because it takes the shape of its container.</u>

3. Think of a way that you could change the ice into water. Write your plan on a separate sheet of paper. Show your plan to your teacher. Once your teacher has approved your plan, try it. Observe and record your results.

   <u>Answers will vary.</u>

Drawing Conclusions

1. How did the properties of the ice change when you tried your plan?

   <u>The ice changed from a hard, cold solid that held its shape to a warmer,</u>

   <u>wet liquid that flowed.</u>

2. How can you tell when something is a solid? A liquid?

   <u>Accept all reasonable responses.</u>

Communicate

Making a Table

When you communicate, you share information with others. Scientists communicate what they learn from an experiment. They might tell people how they think the new information can be used. You can communicate by talking or by creating a drawing, chart, table, or graph.

Communicate what you know about the properties of solids, liquids, and gases. Look at the drawing on this page to help you answer the questions below.

Procedure

1. **Observe** What states of matter do you see in the drawing?

   solid, liquid, gas

2. What properties do these states have?

   Possible answer: Ice is a solid with a definite shape and a definite volume.

   Water is a liquid with a definite volume, but no definite shape. Air is a gas

   with no definite volume or definite shape

3. See the table on the next page.

4. **Communicate** Fill in the table with your observations.

Properties of Matter	
States of Matter	**Properties**
solid	Definite shape and definite volume
liquid	Definite volume, shape changes
gas	Changes shape and volume.

Drawing Conclusions

Communicate Give an example of a solid, a liquid, and a gas. Write a sentence that tells about the shape and volume of each one.

Students should explain that their example of a solid does not change shape or

volume, their example of a liquid changes shape but not volume, and their

example of a gas changes shape and volume.

_____

_____

Explore
Activity
Lesson 3

What Do Magnets Attract?

Hypothesize What kinds of items will be attracted to a magnet? Write a **Hypothesis:**

Possible hypothesis: The objects with metal parts will be

attracted to the magnet.

_____

Materials

• magnet

• several objects

Procedure

1. **Observe** Look at your objects. What properties of the objects do you observe? Record your observations.

   The properties will vary depending on the objects selected.

2. **Predict** Which objects will the magnet attract? Record your predictions.

   The students might predict that metal objects or objects made from iron

   and steel will be attracted to the magnet.

3. **Experiment** Get a magnet from your teacher. Test your predictions. Hold a magnet over each object. Record the results.

   The answers depend upon the objects selected for testing. Most of the

   objects that contain metal will be attracted to the magnet.

Drawing Conclusions

1. **Classify** Use the table below to identify objects the magnet attracts and those objects it does not attract.

Magnet attracts	Magnet does not attract
Items listed as being attracted to the magnet should contain metals.	Most objects listed as not being attracted to the magnet should not contain metals.

Explore Activity
Lesson 3

2. What do the objects that a magnet attracts have in common? What do the objects that a magnet does not attract have in common?

Attracted objects contain some metal. Some objects with metal parts and

non-metallic objects were not attracted to the magnet.

3. FURTHER INQUIRY **Predict** How can magnets be used to separate objects? Test your ideas.

Possible answer: When there is a mixture of objects, a magnet can be used

to separate metal objects from nonmetal objects.

Inquiry

Think of your own questions that you might like to test. Can a magnet be used to separate objects?

My Question Is:

Possible question: Can a magnet attract paper clips in a pile of beads?

How I Can Test It:

Possible test: Test by placing beads in a pile with paper

clips and moving a magnet over the mixture.

My Results Are:

Possible answer: The magnet attracted all of the paper clips.

Treasure Hunt

Procedure

Materials

- small items that will and will not attract a magnet
- large, deep pan of sand
- magnet

1. Observe the objects. Predict whether or not you will be able to find each object using a magnet when the objects are buried in sand. Record your predictions.

   Predictions will vary, but the items made of metal
   should be considered magnetic while all other objects
   should not be considered magnetic.

2. Bury the objects in the sand.

3. Using only the magnet, locate as many buried objects as you can. Record the objects that you find.

   Results will depend on objects.

Drawing Conclusions

1. Which objects did you find with the magnet? Why were you able to find some objects with the magnet but not all?

   Students should be able to find objects made of iron or steel using the
   magnet. They should indicate that only objects attracted to the magnet
   could be found.

2. Compare the objects you found with the magnet. How are they alike?

   They are made wholly or partly of metal.

How Does Heat Affect Different Materials?

Hypothesize You could measure how hot soil and water get when they are exposed to the same amount of heat. Would one type of matter warm up more than the other? How might you test your ideas? Write a **Hypothesis:**

Possible hypothesis: When different types of matter are

exposed to the same amount of heat they do not warm up

an equal amount.

Materials

- soil
- water
- 2 foam cups
- 2 thermometers
- heat source (sunlight or lamp)

Procedure

1. **Predict** Which will heat up faster—a cup of soil or a cup of water?

   Predictions will vary.

2. Fill one cup with water. Fill the other cup with an equal amount of soil.

3. **Measure** Use two thermometers to measure the temperature of the soil and the water. Record the measurements.

   Answers will vary depending on room temperature.

4. **Experiment** Place the soil and water near a heat source. Make sure each cup is the same distance from the heat source. Record the temperature every 5 minutes for 15 minutes in a chart.

   Student findings will vary.

5. **Use Numbers** Find the difference between the first and last readings of each thermometer. To do this, subtract the first measurement you made from the last measurement you made.

   Temperature changes for soil will vary.

© Macmillan/McGraw-Hill

Explore
Activity
Lesson 4

Drawing Conclusions

1. Which cup warmed up more? Were your predictions correct?

   The soil warmed up more. Answers will vary depending on student predictions.

2. **Infer** Why is it important to place the soil and water an equal distance from the heat source?

   The soil and water are placed equal distances from the heat source so that

   they receive the same amount of heat.

3. FURTHER INQUIRY **Experiment** Try this activity using gravel, sand, or salt.

Inquiry

Think of your own questions that you might test. Which would get hotter when they are exposed to the same amount of heat—sand or water?

My Question Is:

Possible question: Does sand heat up faster than water?

How I Can Test It:

Possible test: Prepare a cup of sand and a cup of water. Place both cups by a heat

source and measure the temperature changes.

My Results Are:

Possible answer: Sand will heat up faster than water.

Black and White

Procedure

Materials

- black paper
- white paper
- two ther-
  mometers

1. Cover one thermometer with black paper. Cover the other thermometer with white paper.

2. Place the thermometers in a sunny spot or under a lamp.

3. Predict which thermometer will have a higher reading after 5 minutes. Record your prediction.

   Predictions will vary.
   _____

   _____

4. Wait 5 minutes. Observe and record the thermometer readings.

   Results will vary.
   _____

   _____

Drawing Conclusions

1. Which thermometer had a higher reading? Explain why.

   The thermometer covered with black paper had a higher reading because
   black absorbs heat better than white.

2. What colors would be more comfortable to wear in hot weather? In cold weather?

   light colors; dark colors
   _____

   _____

QUICK LAB

FOR SCHOOL OR HOME

Lesson 4

Expand and Contract

Hypothesize Do gases expand when heated? Do they contract when cooled? Write a **Hypothesis:**

Possible hypothesis: Gases expand when heated and

contract when cooled.

Procedure

1. Stretch the opening of the balloon over a plastic drink bottle.

2. **Observe** Place the bottle in a bucket of warm water. What happens to the balloon? Make a diagram below on the left side.

   The balloon gets bigger.

3. **Observe** Move the bottle to a bucket of cold water. What happens to the balloon? Make a diagram below on the right side.

   The balloon gets smaller.

Materials

- balloon

- 2-L plastic drink bottle

- bucket of warm water

- bucket of cold water

QUICK LAB
FOR SCHOOL OR HOME
Lesson 4

Drawing Conclusions

4. Communicate Explain the changes in the balloon.

When the bottle was placed in warm water the balloon got bigger because

the air warmed up and expanded. When the bottle was placed in cool water

the balloon shrank because the air cooled and contracted.

5. Going Further Does the size of the bottle affect how the balloon expands? Write and conduct an experiment.

My Hypothesis Is:

Possible hypothesis: Using a smaller bottle will make the balloon expand

less than a larger bottle.

My Experiment Is:

Possible experiment: Conduct the same experiment with a smaller

plastic bottle.

My Results Are:

Possible answer: The balloon expanded less when a smaller bottle was

placed in a bucket of warm water.

©Macmillan/McGraw-Hill

● # What Does Light Pass Through?

Hypothesize What kinds of materials can light pass through? How might you test your ideas? Write a **Hypothesis:**

Possible hypothesis: Light passes through materials that are

not opaque.

Materials

- flashlight

- classroom materials, such as paper, wax paper, plastic wrap, aluminum foil, large balloon

Procedure

1. **Predict** Look over your materials. Which materials will light pass through? Which materials will form shadows?

   Answers will vary.

   _____

● 2. **Experiment** Hold each material in front of the lighted flashlight. Does light shine through the material? Do any shadows form? Record your observations.

   The answers depend on the materials selected.

   _____

3. **Experiment** Try changing the materials in some way. You may try folding the papers to make them thicker, or crumpling the plastic wrap. Repeat step 2 with the changed materials.

   The answers will depend on the changes made. Some changes may increase

   the amount of material the light must pass through, decreasing the amount

   of light reaching the student. Other changes may have the opposite effect.

   _____

Drawing Conclusions

1. **Classify** Which materials did the light pass through? Which materials formed shadows? Make a list.

   All transparent materials, such as cellophane, glass, and plastic wrap, allow

   light to pass through. Other materials form shadows.

2. Did changing the materials change the results? Explain any changes you observed.

   Answers will vary depending on the materials selected and the changes

   made to them.

3. **FURTHER INQUIRY** **Predict** How might the brightness of the light affect your results? How do you know?

   Possible answer: Brighter light will pass through material more easily.

Inquiry

Think of your own questions that you might test. What other materials would you like to test?

My Question Is:

Possible question: Can light pass through my hand?

How I Can Test It:

Possible answer: Place my hand in front of the flashlight and move it around.

My Results Are:

Possible answer: Light cannot pass through my hand.

© Macmillan/McGraw-Hill

Window Decorations

Procedure

1. With a partner, plan how you will construct a "stained-glass" decoration to hang in a window. Your decoration must include at least four different materials that allow different amounts of light to pass through them. Be creative in your design. Draw or describe your design on a separate sheet of paper.

2. Use tape to construct your decoration.

3. Use string to hang your decoration in a window.

Materials

- classroom materials, such as paper, wax paper, plastic wrap, aluminum foil

- tape

- string

Drawing Conclusions

Explain your choice of materials for your window decoration.

Student's explanations should include a description of the relative amount of light that passes through the materials.

_____

_____

Use Variables

Controlling an Experiment

Variables are things in an experiment that can be changed to find answers to questions. For example, what if you wanted to answer the question "What affects how light bends in a liquid?" Here are some variables that could be changed:

• the kind of liquid

• the shape of the container

• the position of an object in the liquid

For a fair test, all of the variables in the experiment must remain the same except for one. A variable that does not change is called a control.

Procedure

1. **Communicate** Take a close look at the containers in the picture. What differences do you see? These differences are variables. List all the variables you can on the left side of the table on the next page.

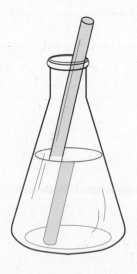

© Macmillan/McGraw-Hill

2. **Use Variables** Describe a fair test for each variable. For example, how would you test the shape of the container?

Possible answer: Use the same size container, the same type and amount of liquid, and the same type of object in the same position. Change only the shape of the container.

Variable	Control
Container	use same size and shape of container
Liquid	use same type and amount of liquid
Object	use same type of object in the same position in the container.

Drawing Conclusions

1. How many variables can you change in a fair test?

One

2. **Use Variables** Which one variable would you change to see its effect on the bending of light? Why?

Possible answer: Students may mention any one of the variables. They should recognize that only one variable at a time should be changed.

How Can You Make Sounds?

Hypothesize There are many different ways that you can make sound. How can you make the sounds change? How might you test your ideas? Write a **Hypothesis:**

Possible hypothesis: To make sounds I can blow through

something or hit something. To change those sounds I can

blow or hit harder or softer.

Materials

- paper strips, 10 cm (4 in.) wide
- tape
- scissors
- straws
- plastic rulers

Procedure: Design Your Own

1. **Observe** Hold a strip of paper at an end. Wave it. Describe what you hear.

   a flapping sound

2. **Observe** Flatten a straw. Cut a point on one end of the straw. Blow hard through that end. Describe what you hear.

   a reedy or honking sound

3. **Observe** Hold a ruler on a desktop. Let half of the ruler reach over the edge. Tap that end. Describe what you hear.

   a thumping or vibrating sound

4. **Experiment** Test ways to change the sound you made with each object. Try to make the sounds louder or quieter, higher or lower. For example, try using strips of paper of different lengths.

   Waving a short strip of paper will produce a higher sound than waving

   a long strip. Blowing into a short straw will produce a higher sound than

   blowing into a long straw. Tapping a short section of a ruler will produce

   a higher sound than tapping a long section. Waving, blowing, and tapping

   with more energy will produce louder sounds.

© Macmillan/McGraw-Hill

Drawing Conclusions

1. What makes sounds?

A moving object makes sounds.

2. How can you make a sound change?

Change the length of the moving object or make the object move with

more energy.

3. FURTHER INQUIRY **Experiment** Make more sound makers out of other materials, such as string and paper cups. How can you change the sounds?

Answers will vary. Possible answers: shorten or lengthen the string or use

cups of different sizes.

Inquiry

Think of your own questions you might like to test. What sound might be made by plucking a long thick rubber band, or a short, thin rubber band?

My Question Is:

What sounds are made by different size rubber bands?

How I Can Test It:

Stretch a rubber band around a box and pluck it.

My Results Are:

long thick rubber band: low sound; short, thin rubber band: high sound

© Macmillan/McGraw-Hill

Changing Sounds

Procedure BE CAREFUL! Wear goggles.

Materials

- box
- rubber band
- pencil
- safety goggles

1. Stretch a rubber band the long way around the box. Then use your fingers to pluck the rubber band. Describe what you hear.

   A low-pitched snappy sound is heard.

2. Next, place a pencil under the rubber band. Pluck the rubber band on one side of the pencil. Describe what you hear.

   The sound now has a higher pitch than before.

Drawing Conclusions

1. What made the sound?

   The vibrating rubber band made the sounds.

2. How did the sound change when a pencil was placed underneath the rubber band?

   Placing a pencil underneath the rubber shortened the vibrating part of the band. Plucking a shorter part of the rubber band made a higher sound.

3. What might happen if you place a second pencil under the rubber band? Why does this happen?

   The vibrating part of the band would be shortened even more. It would make an even higher sound. The shorter the vibrating object is, the higher the pitch of the sound it makes.

© Macmillan/McGraw-Hill

String Phone

Hypothesize Sound travels through the wires of a telephone. How can you use two paper cups, paper clips, and some string to make a telephone? Write a **Hypothesis:**

Possible hypothesis: Like a telephone wire, the string can be used to connect two people. The paper cups can work to focus the sound being produced on one end and to make it loud enough to hear on the other end.

Materials

- 2 paper cups
- string
- 2 paper clips
- tape

Procedure

1. Make a hole in the bottom of a paper cup. Thread 3 meters of string through the hole. Tie the end of the string to a paper clip. Tape the paper clip to the inside of the cup bottom.

2. Repeat step 1. Tie a second paper cup to the other end of the string.

3. **Experiment** Find a partner. Pull the string tight and have your partner listen. Speak softly into the cup. Record your observations.

Answers will vary but should include hearing sounds of the partner speaking.

Drawing Conclusions

4. **Make a Hypothesis** How well will your telephone work if you use a different type of string? Test your ideas.

Students should hypothesize that sound will travel better (or not as well) through a different type of string.

© Macmillan/McGraw-Hill

5. Going Further Does the length of the string affect how well the sound travels? Write and conduct an experiment.

My Hypothesis Is:

Possible hypothesis: the sound does not travel as well with a longer string.

My Experiment Is:

Possible experiment: make two additional cup phones, one with a string shorter than the existing phone and the other with a much longer string. Repeat speaking and listening with a partner and compare how well the sound travels with the short, medium, and long strings.

My Results Are:

Results may vary depending on the material used, but should tend to show that the longer the string length, the less sound reaches the listener.

What Makes the Bulb Light?

Hypothesize You often have to put parts together in a certain way for something to work. How can you put a light bulb, wire, and battery together so that the bulb lights? How might you test your ideas? Write a **Hypothesis:**

Possible hypothesis: The bulb will light if the bulb, battery, and wire are connected.

Materials

- D-cell battery
- small light bulb
- 20-cm wire

Procedure

1. **Predict** Look at the bulb, wire, and battery. How might you put them together to make the bulb light? Work with a partner to record your ideas.

   Possible answer: Run the wire from the bulb's base to one end of the battery and place the bulb's tip on the other end of the battery.

2. **Experiment** Try to light the bulb. Draw a picture of each setup that you try. Record which ones work and which ones don't.

   Encourage students to try different setups using both battery terminals and the base and tip of the bulb.

Drawing Conclusions

1. How many ways did you find to light the bulb?

   Possible answers: There are four possible ways to light the bulb.

2. **Interpret Data** How were the ways that made the bulb light alike? How were they different from the ways that did not make the bulb light?

Possible answer: Each successful setup has to use the wire to connect both ends of the battery with the side and base of the bulb.

Unsuccessful setups were probably missing one or more of these elements.

3. What is the job of the wire?

The wire must touch both the cell and the bulb. The tip or side of the bulb's base must touch the end of the cell opposite the wire.

4. FURTHER INQUIRY **Predict** How could you light the bulb with two pieces of wire?

Use one piece of wire to connect the base of the bulb with one terminal of the cell. Use the other piece to connect the side of the bulb with the other terminal of the cell.

Inquiry

Think of your own questions that you might test. Can you change your setup and still light the bulb?

My Question Is:

Possible question: Students should suggest a different set of connections.

How I Can Test It:

Possible test: Make the suggested connections and see if the bulb lights.

My Results Are:

Possible answer: Either the bulb lit up or it did not, depending on the connections. See the answer to question 2.

© Macmillan/McGraw-Hill

Time's Up!

Procedure

Materials

- D-cell battery
- small electric buzzer
- 20-cm wire

1. Look at the buzzer, wire, and cell. How do you think you might put these three things together to make the buzzer buzz? Record your ideas.

   Accept all reasonable responses.

   _____

   _____

   _____

2. Try to make the buzzer buzz. Draw each setup that you try on a separate sheet of paper. Record which ones work and which ones don't.

   Accept all reasonable responses.

   _____

   _____

Drawing Conclusions

1. How many ways did you find to sound the buzzer? How many ways did you find that did not sound the buzzer? There are four possible ways to sound the buzzer. The possible setups are the same as with the light bulb. The wire, battery, and buzzer must form a loop or circuit.

2. How must the buzzer, wire, and cell be put together so that the buzzer will buzz?

   The buzzer, wire, and cell must form a loop or circuit in order to transfer electricity from the bell to the buzzer.

   _____

Flashlight

Hypothesize A flashlight is a source of light that uses cells as its source of electricity. How can you put the materials together to make a model of a flashlight? Write a **Hypothesis**:

Possible hypothesis: I can make a flashlight by placing the cells in the paper tube so that opposite ends are touching, then connecting the wire to the bulb and to both cells.

Materials

- **2 D cells**
- **paper tube**
- **30 cm wire**
- **masking tape**
- **flashlight bulb**

Procedure

1. Use the materials provided for you to make a model flashlight.

Drawing Conclusions

2. How does your model flashlight work?

   The model flashlight uses cells and a light bulb to produce light.

3. Describe the electric circuit in your flashlight.

   The battery cells create electricity. The electricity flows through the wires to the bulb, which lights when the circuit is closed.

© Macmillan/McGraw-Hill

4. How does your model flashlight compare with a real flashlight?

This model is like a flashlight because it uses the same materials in the

circuit. It is different because there is no switch.

5. **Infer** How might you improve your model?

Add a switch.

6. **Going Further** Electricity can flow through some types of materials but not others. How can you use a circuit to find out whether electricity can flow through certain materials? Write and conduct an experiment.

My Hypothesis Is:

Possible Hypothesis: Electricity can only flow through certain materials.

My Experiment Is:

Possible Experiment: Place a variety of types of materials in the path of the

flashlight circuit. See if the bulb lights. Suggested materials are copper

wire, aluminum foil, string, plastic cord or paper clip, metal paper clip, and

wooden craft stick.

My Results Are:

Answers will vary depending on materials tested. The bulb will light when

copper, aluminum foil, and the metal paper clip are placed in the circuit.

It will not light when the other materials are in the path.